ROMANS

Being a Part of God's Plan

Romans 8-16

Group Directory

Pass this Directory around and have your Group Members
fill in their names and phone numbers

Name   **Phone**

_____   _____

_____   _____

_____   _____

_____   _____

_____   _____

_____   _____

_____   _____

_____   _____

_____   _____

_____   _____

_____   _____

_____   _____

ROMANS

Being a Part of God's Plan

Romans 8-16

EDITING AND PRODUCTION TEAM:
James F. Couch, Jr., Lyman Coleman, Sharon Penington,
Cathy Tardif, Christopher Werner, Matthew Lockhart,
Erika Tiepel, Richard Peace, Andrew Sloan,
Mike Shepherd, Katharine Harris, Scott Lee

NASHVILLE, TENNESSEE

Published by Serendipity House Publishers

Nashville, Tennessee

International Standard Book Number: 1-57494-320-0

ACKNOWLEDGMENTS

Scripture quotations are taken from the Holman Christian Standard Bible,
© Copyright 2000 by Holman Bible Publishers. Used by permission.

03 04 05 06 07 08 / 10 9 8 7 6 5 4 3 2

Nashville, Tennessee

1-800-525-9563

www.serendipityhouse.com

Table of Contents

Core Values

Community: The purpose of this curriculum is to build community within the body of believers around Jesus Christ.

Group Process: To build community, the curriculum must be designed to take a group through a step-by-step process of sharing your story with one another.

Interactive Bible Study: To share your "story," the approach to Scripture in the curriculum needs to be open-ended and right brain—to "level the playing field" and encourage everyone to share.

Developmental Stages: To provide a healthy program throughout the four stages of the life cycle of a group, the curriculum needs to offer courses on three levels of commitment: (1) Beginner Level—low-level entry, high structure, to level the playing field; (2) Growth Level—deeper Bible study, flexible structure, to encourage group accountability; (3) Discipleship Level—in-depth Bible study, open structure, to move the group into high gear.

Target Audiences: To build community throughout the culture of the church, the curriculum needs to be flexible, adaptable and transferable into the structure of the average church.

Mission: To expand the Kingdom of God one person at a time by filling the "empty chair." (We add an extra chair to each group session to remind us of our mission.)

Introduction

Each healthy small group will move through various stages as it matures.

Growth Stage: Here the group begins to care for one another as it learns to apply what they learn through Bible study, worship and prayer.

Develop Stage: The inductive Bible study deepens while the group members discover and develop gifts and skills. The group explores ways to invite their neighbors and coworkers to group meetings.

Birth Stage: This is the time in which group members form relationships and begin to develop community. The group will spend more time in ice-breaker exercises, relational Bible study and covenant building.

Multiply Stage: The group begins the multiplication process. Members pray about their involvement in new groups. The "new" groups begin the life cycle again with the Birth Stage.

 **Subgrouping:** If you have nine or more people at a meeting, Serendipity recommends you divide into subgroups of 3–6 for the Bible study. Ask one person to be the leader of each subgroup and to follow the directions for the Bible study. After 30 minutes, the Group Leader will call "time" and ask all subgroups to come together for the Caring Time.

Each group meeting should include all parts of the "three-part agenda."

Ice-Breaker: Fun, history-giving questions are designed to warm the group and to build understanding about the other group members. You can choose to use all of the Ice-Breaker questions, especially if there is a new group member that will need help in feeling comfortable with the group.

Bible Study: The heart of each meeting is the reading and examination of the Bible. The questions are open, discover questions that lead to further inquiry. Reference notes are provided to give everyone a "level playing field." The emphasis is on understanding what the Bible says and applying the truth to real life. The questions for each session build. There is always at least one "going deeper" question provided. You should always leave time for the last of the "questions for interaction." Should you choose, you can use the optional "going deeper" question to satisfy the desire for the challenging questions in groups that have been together for a while.

Caring Time: All study should point us to actions. Each session ends with prayer and direction in caring for the needs of the group members. You can choose between several questions. You should always pray for the "empty chair." Who do you know that could fill that void in your group?

Sharing Your Story: These sessions are designed for members to share a little of their personal lives each time. Through a number of special techniques each member is encouraged to move from low risk, less personal sharing to higher risk responses. This helps develop the sense of community and facilitates caregiving.

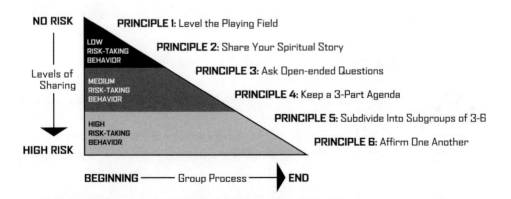

NO RISK

Levels of Sharing

HIGH RISK

LOW RISK-TAKING BEHAVIOR

MEDIUM RISK-TAKING BEHAVIOR

HIGH RISK-TAKING BEHAVIOR

PRINCIPLE 1: Level the Playing Field

PRINCIPLE 2: Share Your Spiritual Story

PRINCIPLE 3: Ask Open-ended Questions

PRINCIPLE 4: Keep a 3-Part Agenda

PRINCIPLE 5: Subdivide Into Subgroups of 3-6

PRINCIPLE 6: Affirm One Another

BEGINNING ——— Group Process ——► END

Group Covenant: A group covenant is a "contract" that spells out your expectations and the ground rules for your group. It's very important that your group discuss these issues—preferably as part of the first session.

GROUND RULES:

- Priority: While you are in the group, you give the group meeting priority.

- Participation: Everyone participates and no one dominates.

- Respect: Everyone is given the right to their own opinion and all questions are encouraged and respected.

- Confidentiality: Anything that is said in the meeting is never repeated outside the meeting.

- Empty Chair: The group stays open to new people at every meeting.

- Support: Permission is given to call upon each other in time of need—even in the middle of the night.

- Advice Giving: Unsolicited advice is not allowed.

- Mission: We agree to do everything in our power to start a new group as our mission.

ISSUES:

- The time and place this group is going to meet is_____

- Refreshments are _____ responsibility.

- Child care is _____ responsibility.

Living in the Spirit

Scripture Romans 8:1–17

Welcome to this study of Romans, chapters 8–16. Together we will learn from one of the richest books of the Bible, considered by many to be the centerpiece of the doctrine of Christianity. Today we begin with the study of chapter 8. Some have said that if the Bible were a wedding ring, Romans would be the diamond and chapter 8 would be the sparkle of that diamond.

 Ice-Breaker Connect With Your Group (15 minutes)

Today we are beginning our journey through Romans with a look at the joyful news that we are God's children and co-heirs with Christ. We also rejoice that the Holy Spirit lives in us and helps us to make the right choices. Take some time to get to know one another better by sharing your responses to the following questions.

1. What heirloom would you like to pass along to your family someday?

2. Who were your best friends in high school? Did they ever convince you to do something mischievous you didn't want to do? What happened?

3. Who or what most influences your decision making today?

   ○ Values.
   ○ Family.
   ○ Education.
   ○ Current events.
   ○ Other _____.

Leader
Be sure to read the introductory material in the front of this book prior to this first session. To help your group members get acquainted, have each person introduce him or herself and then take turns answering one or two of the Ice-Breaker questions. If time allows, you may want to discuss all three questions.

Bible Study Read Scripture and Discuss (30 minutes)

The result of Christ's work on the cross for the believer is that we cannot be condemned for our sins. However, that does not mean our battle with sin doesn't continue to rage. To help us fight this daily battle, God has not left us alone; he has given us the Holy Spirit. Read Romans 8:1–17 and note how the Holy Spirit helps us in our weakness and fear.

Leader
Select a member of the group ahead of time to read aloud the Scripture passage. Then discuss the Questions for Interaction, dividing into subgroups of three to six. Be sure to save time at the end for the Caring Time.

Living in the Spirit

8 Therefore, no condemnation now exists for those in Christ Jesus, ²because the Spirit's law of life in Christ Jesus has set you free from the law of sin and of death. ³What the law could not do since it was limited by the flesh, God did. He condemned sin in the flesh by sending His own Son in flesh like ours under sin's domain, and as a sin offering, ⁴in order that the law's requirement would be accomplished in us who do not walk according to the flesh but according to the Spirit. ⁵For those whose lives are according to the flesh think about the things of the flesh, but those whose lives are according to the Spirit, about the things of the Spirit. ⁶For the mind-set of the flesh is death, but the mind-set of the Spirit is life and peace. ⁷For the mind-set of the flesh is hostile to God because it does not submit itself to God's law, for it is unable to do so. ⁸Those whose lives are in the flesh are unable to please God. ⁹You, however, are not in the flesh, but in the Spirit, since the Spirit of God lives in you. But if anyone does not have the Spirit of Christ, he does not belong to Him. ¹⁰Now if Christ is in you, the body is dead because of sin, but the Spirit is life because of righteousness. ¹¹And if the Spirit of Him who raised Jesus from the dead lives in you, then He who raised Christ from the dead will also bring your mortal bodies to life through His Spirit who lives in you.

¹²So then, brothers, we are not obligated to the flesh to live according to the flesh, ¹³for if you live according to the flesh, you are going to die. But if by the Spirit you put to death the deeds of the body, you will live. ¹⁴All those led by God's Spirit are God's sons. ¹⁵For you did not receive a spirit of slavery to fall back into fear, but you received the Spirit of adoption, by whom we cry out, "*Abba*, Father!" ¹⁶The Spirit Himself testifies together with our spirit that we are God's children, ¹⁷and if children, also heirs—heirs of God and co-heirs with Christ—seeing that we suffer with Him so that we may also be glorified with Him.

Romans 8:1–17

Questions for Interaction

Leader
Refer to the Summary and Study Notes at the end of this session as needed. If 30 minutes is not enough time to answer all of the questions in this section, conclude the Bible Study by answering questions 6 and 7.

1. What part of your budget is the hardest to follow and stay within your spending limit?

   ○ Food.
   ○ Clothing.
   ○ Entertainment.
   ○ Christmas gifts.
   ○ Nothing. I'm always in control of my spending.
   ○ Other _____.

2. From verses 1–4, how would you explain the Gospel to someone who feels he is not "good enough" for God?

3. What are some examples of "things of the flesh" and "things of the Spirit" (v. 5)? Where is the battle for control of your life (flesh vs. the Spirit) going to be fought and won (vv. 6–8)?

4. According to verse 11, the Holy Spirit raised Jesus from the dead on the third day and that same Spirit dwells within us. What are the implications of having this power source in our lives on a daily basis?

5. From this passage, what roles do God, Jesus and the Holy Spirit play in setting you free?

6. What is the hardest part for you about yielding to the Holy Spirit's power? When unhealthy thoughts and desires enter your mind, what have you found helpful in dealing with them?

7. As an adopted child of God, you have access to all the privileges of an heir. What does it mean to you to be adopted by God as his child?

Going Deeper   If your group has time and/or wants a challenge, go on to this question.

8. How has the Spirit borne witness with your spirit that you are a child of God? What are some ways we suffer with Christ (v. 17)?

Caring Time Apply the Lesson and Pray for One Another (15 minutes)

This very important time is for developing and expressing your concern for each other as group members by praying for one another.

1. Agree on the group covenant and ground rules that are described in the introduction to this book.

2. How can we encourage one another to yield daily to the power of the Holy Spirit who lives within us? Are we available if a group member needs us in the "middle of the night"?

3. Share any other prayer requests and praises, and then close in prayer. Pray specifically for God to lead you to someone to bring next week to fill the empty chair.

Leader
Take some extra time in this first session to go over the introductory material at the front of this book. At the close, pass around your books and have everyone sign the Group Directory, also found in the front of this book.

NEXT WEEK *Today we saw how the Holy Spirit provides the power and help to overcome the daily battles of our flesh. However, it is one thing to know these truths; it is quite another to appropriate them. We must not operate in fear, as verse 15 mentions, but we should encourage one another to yield the mind, will, emotions and body to the Holy Spirit daily. Pick a group member to pray for in the coming week, that he or she would be open to the power of the Holy Spirit and be able to overcome sin. Also, call that person during the week and offer some words of encouragement. Next week we will look at the amazing love God has for people and how nothing can separate us from that love.*

Notes on Romans 8:1–17

Summary: Paul sums up his case: While the Law is good and holy and reflects accurately God's mind and will, in the end it is only words and propositions; i.e., it has no inherent life or power. It can tell one what to do, but it cannot enable anyone to do it. Since human personality is infected with sin and destined to failure, two things are required: forgiveness for past and present failure (Christ's sin offering), and a new inner dynamic that enables humans to subdue sin (the Holy Spirit). To live according to the Spirit is to live in a way that reflects the character of God rather than that of sin.

8:1 *no condemnation.* Christians are free from both the guilt which sin produces (and hence have no anxiety about being condemned on the future Day of Judgment), and are free from the total enslaving power of sin (and hence can live in God's way in the here and now).

8:2 *the Spirit's.* This is the Holy Spirit, the third person of the Trinity, who indwells believers in power. In chapter 8, Paul will refer to the Spirit over 20 times—more references to the Spirit than in any other single chapter of the New Testament. *set you free.* There is at work in believers a power greater than sin—a power that enables them to resist sin effectively. They are no longer willing (or unwilling) slaves of sin. Rather, they are living between the pressure to sin and the greater Spirit-induced pressure to resist. Their new ability to resist is the pledge that one day they will be completely free from the authority of sin.

8:3 *flesh*. Human nature in its vulnerability to sin was unable to keep God's Law. Hence, the Law could not save anyone. In response to this plight, Christ, as God's representative, bore the punishment of sin in place of those who deserved it. ***like ours*.** Jesus took on weak human nature, but it was not to the exclusion of his divine nature. He was fully God and fully man.

8:5 *lives are according to*. There are two options: to be preoccupied with sinful desires or to be focused on the desires of the Holy Spirit. ***think about*.** This includes assumptions, values, outlook, desires, purpose—all that forms one's perspective on life. What a person thinks determines how that person acts.

8:6 *death/life*. The two outlooks lead to two patterns of conduct that result in two spiritual states—death to God (because sin separates one from him) or life in the Spirit.

8:9 The distinguishing characteristic of the Christian is the indwelling of the Holy Spirit.

8:10–11 The consequence of having the Spirit within a person is life: life now (v. 10) and life eventually for the mortal body (v. 11), when the Christian experiences bodily resurrection.

8:12 Grammatically, it appears that Paul originally intended to complete the sentence by saying that not only do believers have no obligation to the flesh but they do have an obligation to the

Spirit to live according to it. Yet having stated the negative, he breaks off in mid-sentence to add the warning found in verse 13a. Once launched in this direction he balances off this statement in 13a by his assertion in verse 13b. But he then fails to complete the sentence begun in verse 12! ***obligated*.** Christians have no further obligation to indulge their self-centeredness. Rather, they owe a debt to a life of holiness; i.e., they are obliged to live a life that is consistent with the life of the Spirit within them.

8:13 *put to death*. In Romans 7:4 Paul says that Christians are "put to death in relation to the law" through Christ's once-for-all act of dying on the cross in their place. In response to this fact, believers are daily (the verb tense indicates an action that is repeated over and over) to "put to death" all those practices they know to be wrong, all the attitudes that are not of God, and all the thoughts that would lead to sin. The presence of the Holy Spirit in one's life is not the end of the battle against sin but only the beginning, in the sense that now there is a hope of winning (Matt. 16:24; Gal. 5:24). ***you will live*.** That is, this is the evidence that one has truly come to Christ and thus has the promise of eternal life.

8:15 *spirit of slavery*. The Holy Spirit brings one, not into a new form of anxious bondage, but rather unites one with Christ, enabling one to share his sonship. ***you received*.** The verb tense indicates that this is a one-time, past action—something that happened at conversion. ***adoption*.** The Roman practice of adoption was a most serious and complicated process, because a child was the absolute possession of his father (the father had the legal right to even kill his child). For a boy to be adopted into a new family, he was first symbolically "sold" by his father to the adopting father. Then the legal case for adoption was taken to the magistrate. ***cry*.** In the Psalms this word is used of urgent prayer (Ps. 3:4). ***Abba*.** An Aramaic word used by children;

best translated "Daddy," signifying a close, intimate relationship. *Abba, Father!* The very words Jesus prayed in the Garden of Gethsemane (Mark 14:36).

8:16 In the Roman adoptive proceedings there were several witnesses to the ceremony who would, if a dispute arose later, verify that the particular child had actually been adopted. The Holy Spirit is the one who verifies a person's adoption into the family of God.

8:17 *heirs.* If someone is one of God's children, then that person is an heir, and will share in God's riches. In fact, Jesus is God's true heir (v. 3), but since believers are "in Christ," they become sons and daughters of God by adoption (and so use the same words to address God as Jesus did), and thus are joint-heirs with Christ. *suffer.* The willingness to suffer for Christ is a mark of belonging. *be glorified.* Christians have the hope of sharing in the reign of Christ over all creation.

Nothing Can Separate Us From God's Love

Scripture Romans 8:18–39

LAST WEEK *In last week's session, we looked at how the Holy Spirit gives us the power to overcome the daily battles of our flesh. We considered how we must yield the mind, will, emotions and body to the Holy Spirit daily, and not let fear overtake us. Today we are going to focus on the awesome love God has for us, and how absolutely nothing can take that love away from us. We will also be encouraged by God's provision of the Holy Spirit to intercede for us.*

 Ice-Breaker Connect With Your Group (15 minutes)

Paul lifts our spirits today by reminding us of the future glory awaiting those who follow Christ, and of the incredible love of God. Take turns sharing your thoughts and unique life experiences with finding hope and love.

Leader
Begin the session with a word of prayer. Have your group members take turns sharing their responses to one, two or all three of the Ice-Breaker questions. Be sure that everyone gets a chance to participate.

1. When you daydream, where do you catch yourself going?

   ○ To the majestic mountains.
   ○ To a sunny beach.
   ○ To a hammock swaying in the breeze.
   ○ To a solitary boat floating on the lake.
   ○ Other _____.

2. When you have a bad day, what lifts your spirits?

3. What other human being(s) do you love more than yourself?

Bible Study Read Scripture and Discuss (30 minutes)

The desire of every human being is to be loved by someone. As this passage teaches, God's love for us is so wonderful it can't even be compared to human love. Sure we could sacrifice our life for another. Soldiers in time of war have proven that. But we do not have the power to bring that sacrificed life back from the dead. Paul writes that God's love is so great, it cannot be separated from us even when we die. Let's read of this love and our future glory in Romans 8:18–39.

Leader
Select two members of the group ahead of time to read aloud the Scripture passage. Have one person read verses 18–27; and the other read verses 28–39. Then discuss the Questions for Interaction, dividing into subgroups of three to six.

Nothing Can Separate Us From God's Love

Reader 1: [18]For I consider that the sufferings of this present time are not worth comparing with the glory that is going to be revealed to us. [19]For the creation eagerly waits with anticipation for God's sons to be revealed. [20]For the creation was subjected to futility—not willingly, but because of Him who subjected it—in the hope [21]that the creation itself will also be set free from the bondage of corruption into the glorious freedom of God's children. [22]For we know that the whole creation has been groaning together with labor pains until now. [23]And not only that, but we ourselves who have the Spirit as the firstfruits—we also groan within ourselves, eagerly waiting for adoption, the redemption of our bodies. [24]Now in this hope we were saved, yet hope that is seen is not hope, because who hopes for what he sees? [25]But if we hope for what we do not see, we eagerly wait for it with patience. [26]In the same way the Spirit also joins to help in our weakness, because we do not know what to pray for as we should, but the Spirit Himself intercedes for us with unspoken groanings. [27]And He who searches the hearts knows the Spirit's mind-set, because He intercedes for the saints according to the will of God.

Reader 2: [28]We know that all things work together for the good of those who love God: those who are called according to His purpose. [29]For those He foreknew He also predestined to be conformed to the image of His Son, so that He would be the firstborn among many brothers. [30]And those He predestined, He also called; and those He called, He also justified; and those He justified, He also glorified.

[31]What then are we to say about these things?
If God is for us, who is against us?
[32]He did not even spare His own Son,
but offered Him up for us all;
how will He not also with Him grant us everything?
[33]Who can bring an accusation against God's elect?
God is the One who justifies.
[34]Who is the one who condemns?
Christ Jesus is the One who died, but even more, has been raised;

He also is at the right hand of God and intercedes for us.
³⁵Who can separate us from the love of Christ?
Can affliction or anguish or persecution
or famine or nakedness or danger or sword?
³⁶As it is written:
Because of You we are being put to death all day long;
we are counted as sheep to be slaughtered.
³⁷No, in all these things we are more than victorious
through Him who loved us.
³⁸For I am persuaded that neither death nor life,
nor angels nor rulers,
nor things present, nor things to come, nor powers,
³⁹nor height, nor depth, nor any other created thing
will have the power to separate us
from the love of God that is in Christ Jesus our Lord!

Romans 8:18–39

Questions for Interaction

Leader
Refer to the Summary and Study Notes at the end of this session as needed. If 30 minutes is not enough time to answer all of the questions in this section, conclude the Bible Study by answering question 7.

1. What do you think heaven is like?

2. What is it that you hope for in this life? What about in the life to come?

   ○ Peace on earth.
   ○ Suffering to end.
   ○ Evil to be punished.
   ○ Relationships to be restored.
   ○ Other _____.

3. What does Paul mean by the "glory that is going to be revealed" (v. 18)?

4. What is creation "groaning" about (v. 22)? What are Christians groaning about according to verse 23? What are we hoping for?

5. What does the Holy Spirit do for us when we don't know how to pray? How does that make you feel?

6. When have you had a hard time believing the truth of verse 28?

7. Even though you know how much God loves you, have there been times when you felt separated from him? What situation has recently caused you to feel that way? What phrase from verses 31–39 is a comfort to you right now in your journey?

8. What does Paul mean by "foreknew" in verse 29? What is the progression for the follower of Christ as described in this verse? What does it mean? How can we be encouraged by it?

Caring Time   Apply the Lesson and Pray for One Another   (15 minutes)

Take some time now to encourage and support one another in a time of sharing and prayer. Remember that the Spirit is interceding for you and helps you to pray.

Leader
Bring the group members back together and begin the Caring Time by sharing responses to all three questions. Then take turns sharing prayer requests and have a time of group prayer.

1. This last week, did you feel more defeated or victorious? Why?

2. In what area of your life do you especially need the Spirit's intercession in the coming week?

3. What would you like to thank God for regarding his unconditional love for you?

    P.S. *Add new group members to the Group Directory at the front of this book.*

NEXT WEEK *Today we considered the future glory that awaits those who follow Christ, and we were assured that nothing can separate us from God's love. We were also encouraged by God's provision of the Holy Spirit to intercede for us. In the coming week, think of special ways to show God how much you appreciate his love. Next week we will look at Paul's concern for the Jewish people.*

Summary: The transition in Paul's thought from the former section (8:1–17) to this new section (8:18–39) really occurs at verse 17, where his focus shifts from the fact that Christians are the children of God to the fact that Christians are the heirs of God. The idea of inheritance leads to the theme of verses 18–27: the hope that people have whom the Spirit of God indwells. In 8:28–39, a well-known and well-loved section of Romans, Paul tells the reader why it is that he can dismiss present suffering as "not worth comparing with the glory that is going to be revealed in us" (8:18). In these verses he reveals the basis for the sense of hope he has (which he just described in 8:17–27). In one of his most eloquent passages (8:31–35), Paul hurls a challenge out to all who would oppose believers: Absolutely nothing can separate Christians from God's love.

8:18 *I consider.* This could be translated, "I reckon." Paul has used this same Greek word in 3:28 ("we maintain") and in 6:11 ("count"). In each case, he means by it a firm conviction that can be worked out logically from the Gospel message. *sufferings/glory.* Paul defines the basic contrast that will be the subject of verses 18–27. His point: one's future glory (inheritance) vastly outweighs one's present distress (sufferings). *sufferings.* That is, the persecutions that Christians face in the time between Jesus' first coming and his return. These are slight in comparison with the glory ahead.

8:19 *eagerly waits with anticipation.* The image is of a person with excited anticipation scanning the horizon for the first sign of the coming dawn of glory. The only other occurrence of this word in the New Testament is in Philippians 1:20. *for God's sons to be revealed.* Christians are indeed sons and daughters of God here and now in this life. What Paul refers to here is the fact that they are, as it were, incognito. It will only be at the Second Coming that it will be revealed for all to see who are, in fact, the children of God.

8:20 *For.* Verses 20–21 explain why the creation waits with such eagerness for this revealing. *the creation.* This includes the whole of the nonhuman world, both living and inanimate. *was subjected.* The verb tense indicates a single past action (Gen. 3:17–19). *futility.* The inability of creation to achieve the goal for which it was created—that of glorifying God—because the key actor in this drama of praise (mankind) has fallen. This word is also translated "vanity," and is used extensively in the book of Ecclesiastes. *in the hope.* There was divine judgment at the Fall, but this was not without hope. One day, it was said, the woman's offspring would crush the serpent's head (Gen. 3:15).

8:21 *will also be set free.* Creation will be freed from its frustrating bondage at the time of the Second Coming when the children of God are freed from the last vestiges of sin. *bondage of corruption.* All of creation seems to be running down; deterioration and decomposition now characterize the created order.

8:22 *labor pains.* Such pain is very real, very intense, but also temporary (and the necessary prelude to new life). The image is not of the annihilation of the present universe, but of the emergence of a transformed order (Rev. 21:1). Childbirth was a Jewish metaphor for the suffering that would precede the coming of the new age (Isa. 26:17).

8:23 *firstfruits.* Generally this term refers to those early developing pieces of fruit that were harvested and given to God, but here the idea is of a gift from God to people. The experience by the believer of the work of the Holy Spirit is a pledge that one day God will grant all that he has promised. *we ... groan within.* One groans not just because of persecution, but because one is not yet fully redeemed. Believers' bodies are still subject to weakness, pain and death. The believer therefore longs for the suffering to end and for the redemption of the body to be complete. *eagerly waiting.* In one sense Christians are already adopted children of God, but in another sense they have yet to fully experience their inheritance.

8:26–27 Human frailty affects even prayer. Sometimes feelings are so deep and so inexpressible that it is the Holy Spirit himself who must pray for an individual.

8:28 *all things work together.* It is God who takes that which is adverse and painful (the groans, the persecution and even death—see vv. 35–36) and brings profit out of it. *for the good of those who love God.* This does not mean that things work out so that believers preserve their comfort and convenience. Rather, such action on God's part enables these difficult experiences to assist in the process of salvation. *those who are called according to His purpose.* The love people have for God is a reflection of the fact and reality of God's love for them as expressed in his call to individuals to follow Christ. In fact, a person's love for God can even be said to be a proof of God's love for that person. Had God not called an individual, that person would still be his enemy and unable and unwilling to love him.

8:29 *foreknew.* God knew even before the world was created who would have faith (Eph. 1:4; 2 Tim. 1:9). In the Old Testament, the word "knew" carried the idea of "knowing" in a relational sense. To know someone is to be in relationship with that person (and not simply to know facts about him or her). For God to know someone is for him to love and have a purpose for that person. *predestined.* God puts into effect what he foreknew. His purpose for people, as spelled out in the next phrase, is Christlikeness or holiness. *conformed to the image.* Behind this phrase lies the Old Testament concept of a man and woman being made in the image of God (Gen. 1:27), and Christ who is the very image of God (2 Cor. 4:4). While Paul has in mind that time of glorification (when believers will be brought into full conformity to the image of Christ), he is probably also thinking of ongoing sanctification, whereby believers come ever closer to the image of Christ (through daily suffering and obedience). *firstborn among many.* The image is of Jesus as the elder son among many family members (who have come via adoption).

8:30 *called.* Foreknowledge and predestination are prerogatives of God that enter the realm of history at the point of calling, whereby one hears the Gospel and responds in faith. The end result then is justification.

8:38 *death/life.* For Paul, to die was no longer a threat—it was to "be with Christ" (Phil. 1:21–23). Life is used here in the sense of trials, distractions and enticements that could easily lead one away from God. *present/things to come.* Neither this age nor the events in the future eschatological age are to be feared.

8:39 *height/depth.* These words were used in first-century astrology to signify spirits that ruled in the sky above or below the horizon. Or the reference could be to the influence of a star at the height or the depth of its zenith. It may mean simply that neither heaven nor hell can separate Christians from God's love.

Paul's Concern for the Jewish People

Scripture Romans 9:1–24

LAST WEEK *God's amazing love for us was our topic for last week's session. We were assured that there is absolutely nothing that can separate us from that perfect, unconditional love. We were also reminded that the Holy Spirit intercedes for us and helps us to pray. Today we will look at Paul's concern for the Jewish people. He longed for them to accept what Jesus did for them, and he wanted them to accept God's plan of salvation for the Gentiles as well.*

 Ice-Breaker Connect With Your Group (15 minutes)

Leader
Choose one or two Ice-Breaker questions. If you have a new group member you may want to do all three. Remember to stick closely to the three-part agenda and the time allowed for each segment.

A sense of belonging is something we all strive for. It helps us to know that we're not alone and there are others who share our background and values. The Jewish people in Paul's day enjoyed this sense of being God's chosen people, and they didn't exactly like the idea of sharing this distinction. Take turns sharing how you have "belonged" to others in your life.

1. What did you and your siblings or friends fight about the most when growing up?

   ○ What to watch on TV.
   ○ Chore assignments.
   ○ What to play.
   ○ Room territory.
   ○ Other _____.

2. What teams, groups, clubs or organizations are you a member of? Is there an initiation to get into your group? What is it?

3. What is something interesting about your family's background?

Bible Study Read Scripture and Discuss (30 minutes)

Leader
Ask two members of the group, selected ahead of time, to read aloud the Scripture passage. Have one person read verses 1–14 and the other person read verses 15–24. Then discuss the Questions for Interaction, dividing into subgroups of three to six.

In this passage, Paul reminds the Jewish people of all that God has blessed them with, including the fact that from them is traced the human ancestry of Jesus. He blessed them in ways he blessed no other group of people. But they now needed to accept that God sent his son Jesus to make it possible for the Gentiles to also receive those blessings. Read Romans 9:1–24 and see how the Jews react to sharing their blessings.

Paul's Concern for the Jewish People

9 I speak the truth in Christ—I am not lying; my conscience is testifying to me with the Holy Spirit— ²that I have intense sorrow and continual anguish in my heart. ³For I could wish that I myself were cursed and cut off from the Messiah for the benefit of my brothers, my countrymen by physical descent. ⁴They are Israelites, and to them belong the adoption, the glory, the covenants, the giving of the law, the temple service, and the promises. ⁵The forefathers are theirs, and from them, by physical descent, came the Messiah, who is God over all, blessed forever. Amen.

⁶But it is not as though the word of God has failed. For not all who are descended from Israel are Israel. ⁷Neither are they all children because they are Abraham's descendants. On the contrary, in Isaac your seed will be called. ⁸That is, it is not the children by physical descent who are God's children, but the children of the promise are considered seed. ⁹For this is the statement of the promise: At this time I will come, and Sarah will have a son. ¹⁰And not only that, but also when Rebekah became pregnant by Isaac our forefather ¹¹(for though they had not been born yet or done anything good or bad, so that God's purpose according to election might stand, ¹²not from works but from the One who calls) she was told: The older will serve the younger. ¹³As it is written: Jacob I have loved, but Esau I have hated.

¹⁴What should we say then? Is there injustice with God? Absolutely not! ¹⁵For He tells Moses:
I will show mercy to whom I show mercy,
and I will have compassion on whom I have compassion.
¹⁶So then it does not depend on human will or effort, but on God who shows mercy. ¹⁷For the Scripture tells Pharaoh:
For this reason I raised you up:
so that I may display My power in you,
and that My name may be proclaimed in all the earth.
¹⁸So then, He shows mercy to whom He wills, and He hardens whom He wills.
¹⁹You will say to me, therefore, "Why then does He still find fault? For who can resist His will?"
²⁰But who are you—anyone who talks back to God? Will what is formed say to the one who formed it, "Why did you make me like this?" ²¹Or has the potter no right over His clay, to make from the same lump one piece of pottery for honor and another for dishonor? ²²And what if God, desiring to display His wrath and to make His power known, endured with much patience objects of

wrath ready for destruction? [23]And what if He did this to make known the riches of His glory on objects of mercy that He prepared beforehand for glory— [24]on us whom He also called, not only from the Jews but also from the Gentiles?

Romans 9:1–24

Questions for Interaction

Leader
Refer to the Summary and Study Notes at the end of this session as needed. If 30 minutes is not enough time to answer all of the questions in this section, conclude the Bible Study by answering question 7.

1. Have you ever won anything in a contest or been given an award? If so, what were you given? How did it feel to be chosen?

2. Who would you be willing to be "cursed" for to assure that person's salvation?

   ○ Parents.
   ○ Neighbors.
   ○ Spouse.
   ○ Children.
   ○ Other _____.

3. According to verse 5, what are some special blessings given to the Jews? How did Paul want the Jews to respond to God?

4. According to verses 6–13, who are the children of God? What is the process to become a child of God? Why does God reject some and show mercy to others?

5. Paul is making his case to the Jews that God has accepted the Gentles who believe. Why were the Jews rejecting that?

6. What is your response when you realize that God made a way for you to come to the truth? What would you say to God if you could meet him face-to-face?

7. What will you do with your life as a result of God choosing you to be one of his children and follow in his ways?

Going Deeper   If your group has time and/or wants a challenge, go on to this question.

8. According to verses 14–24, who are some people God has rejected? Who has he accepted? Is he an unjust God for doing so?

Caring Time Apply the Lesson and Pray for One
Another (15 minutes)

Leader
Begin the Caring Time by having group members take turns sharing responses to all three questions. Be sure to save at least the last five minutes for a time of group prayer. Remember to include a prayer for the empty chair when concluding the prayer time.

Encouraging and supporting each other is especially vital if this group is to become all it can be. Take time now to share God's mercy and compassion and pray for one another.

1. On a scale of 1 (I'm incognito) to 10 (I'm an open book), how would you rate the degree that other people can tell you are one of God's children? How would you like that to change?

2. What do you appreciate about belonging to this group? How could you support one another in the coming week?

3. Name two or three blessings that you would like to thank God for.

NEXT WEEK *Today we looked at Paul's concern for the Jewish people and how he longed that they would accept what Jesus did for them. He also hoped that they would accept God's plan to welcome Gentiles who believed in Jesus. We were reminded of how God has blessed us, and how privileged we are to be his children. In the coming week, ask the Holy Spirit to give you boldness in sharing God's plan of salvation with someone. Next week, we will look at Israel's rejection of Jesus and see how Paul shares the Gospel with those who don't believe.*

Summary: Paul begins his argument by affirming the special privileges given the people of Israel (vv. 1–5). Then he points out that to be a member of the true Israel has never been a matter of natural descent. Rather, it is a question of election—God's process of selection has nothing to do with merit or right (vv. 6–13). Finally, Paul addresses the question, "Is God unjust?" (vv. 14–24).

9:3 *cursed.* Literally, "anathema." When something was declared anathema, it was given over to God for total destruction. *cut off from the Messiah.* The horror of Paul's wish becomes clear. He who has written with such passion and delight about the Christian's glorification would renounce even this, his final salvation, for the sake of his own people (Ex. 32:32).

9:4 *Israelites.* The special name given by God to Jacob and his descendants who were to be a special people to God. *adoption.* Israel has a special relationship with God. He is their Father, they are his children (Ex. 4:22; Deut. 14:1). The use of the word adoption calls attention to the fact that this relationship is by grace—a product of God's action and not the result of natural succession. *glory.* The supernatural light which was present when God made his presence known to Israel (Ex. 16:10)—the visible presence of the invisible God. *covenants.* The formal agreements signifying a special relationship between God and Israel. He would be their God and they his people who would serve him (Gen. 15:17–18; Ex. 19:5–6). *the law.* That in which God's will had been made known. *temple service.* Through the sacrificial system, Israel had special access to God. *promises.* Old Testament prophecies that stressed that God had a great and noble task in store for Israel.

9:5 *forefathers.* The original leaders of Israel: Abraham, Isaac, Jacob and Jacob's 12 sons. *physical descent.* All this led up to the coming of the Messiah—God's own Son who was born into the world as a Jew. *who is God.* Jesus is, in fact, God—the divine Lord over all creation.

9:11 *God's purpose according to election.* This is the key issue in chapters 9–11.

9:12–13 These quotations from Genesis 25:23 and Malachi 1:2–3 apply not to two people (Jacob and Esau), but to two tribes (Jews and Edomites) who descended from them. God selected one tribe through whom to develop his plan of salvation, and the other tribe (by not having been elected) was excluded from this particular purpose.

9:13 *loved/hated.* These words express election and rejection (inclusion and exclusion), not an emotional reaction on God's part. As with Ishmael, Esau also remained an object of God's mercy, if not his purposeful plan. Thus, Paul points out that many Jews are, in fact, like Ishmael and Esau—objects of God's mercy, but outside the circle of those in whom God's purpose is expressed.

9:14 Having shown that God's dealing with Israel has been consistent since the time of Abraham, Paul must now show that such dealings have not been unjust. This is especially crucial, since a key theme of Romans is God's righteousness (or justice).

9:15–16 Paul uses this verse from Exodus 33:19 to show the freedom of God's mercy. Individuals cannot by virtue of works or parentage insist that he give mercy to them and not to others. God is free to offer such mercy (i.e., active, outgoing compassion) to whomever he chooses.

9:17 *Pharaoh.* The ruler of Egypt (who enslaved Israel at the time of the Exodus) is an example of those who resist God—as unbelieving Israel is now doing. The issue is not the personal fate of Pharaoh, but how God used his opposition. ***My power.*** The focus is not on God's unlimited might, but as in Romans 1:16 (and in 1 Cor. 6:14) on God's saving power which is sufficient to deliver his people from slavery. ***My name.*** God's character is revealed in his acts, and so his deliverance of Israel from Pharaoh becomes known all over the world.

9:18 *mercy ... hardens.* God has mercy on some, in that he allows them consciously and voluntarily to serve his purpose. Others he hardens, in the sense that they have a negative role to play. In the Old Testament, while it says that God hardened Pharaoh's heart, it also says that Pharaoh had already hardened his own heart (Ex. 8:15). ***He wills.*** God's will is not inconsistent and arbitrary. As verse 15 indicates, it is constrained by mercy.

9:19 The hypothetical opponent raises two obvious objections. If God's will cannot be resisted, should a person (e.g., Pharaoh) then be held responsible for what that person, in fact, had no choice but to do?

9:20–21 God is free to appoint people to various tasks for his overall place and purpose. But just as a potter is not impulsive (he makes what he can sell), God has a purpose for even a stubborn Pharaoh and unbelieving Israel (as he shows in vv. 22–24).

9:22 *patience.* Though unbelieving Israel deserved punishment (the Old Testament recounts their continual rebellion against God), God was patient with them because from them Jesus would come. ***objects of wrath.*** This does not mean they will always be such. God's patience may indeed lead to their repentance.

9:23 *make known the riches of His glory.* This is the ultimate purpose for God's endurance of Pharaoh and a rebellious Israel. In Romans 9:30–11:36 it becomes clear that such divine patience has the effect of revealing the baseness of sin out of which emerges the salvation of rebel Israel.

Israel's Rejection of Jesus

Scripture Romans 9:30–10:4

LAST WEEK *In last week's session, we looked at Paul's concern for the Jewish people and how he longed that they would accept Jesus as the Messiah. He even wished himself to be cursed if it would save his own people. He also hoped that they would accept Gentile believers as part of God's plan of salvation. Today we continue with a look at why Israel rejects Jesus and what they are trusting in for their salvation.*

 Ice-Breaker Connect With Your Group (15 minutes)

Most of us have worked very hard for what we have, so sometimes it's difficult to understand how God can just give us our salvation as a gift. Take turns sharing some of your thoughts and experiences with working hard.

Leader
Choose one, two or all three of the Ice-Breaker questions. Welcome and introduce new group members.

1. What have you worked hard to obtain? What "stumbling stones" did you encounter along the way?

   ○ Getting my college degree.
   ○ Buying a house.
   ○ Raising my children.
   ○ Getting a promotion.
   ○ Other _____.

2. What did you have "zeal for" in high school?

  ○ Girls/Guys.
  ○ Math.
  ○ Science.
  ○ English.
  ○ Sports.
  ○ Skipping class.
  ○ Other _____.

3. If you could have one wish or "heart's desire" granted by God, what would it be?

Bible Study Read Scripture and Discuss (30 minutes)

No one likes to be rejected. But Jesus is rejected on a daily basis. It started many years ago with the very people he came to save. As you read Romans 9:30–10:4, think of the people you know who have rejected God. Ask God to make your heart ache for them.

Leader
Have a member of the group, selected ahead of time, read aloud the Scripture passage. Then discuss the Questions for Interaction, dividing into subgroups of three to six.

Israel's Rejection of Jesus

³⁰What should we say then? Gentiles, who did not pursue righteousness, have obtained righteousness—namely the righteousness that comes from faith. ³¹But Israel, pursuing the law for righteousness, has not achieved the law. ³²Why is that? Because they did not pursue it by faith, but as if it were by works. They stumbled over the stumbling stone. ³³As it is written:

Look! I am putting a stone in Zion to stumble over,
and a rock to trip over,
yet the one who believes on Him will not be put to shame.

10 Brothers, my heart's desire and prayer to God concerning them is for their salvation! ²I can testify about them that they have zeal for God, but not according to knowledge. ³Because they disregarded the righteousness from God and attempted to establish their own righteousness, they have not submitted to God's righteousness. ⁴For Christ is the end of the law for righteousness to everyone who believes.

Romans 9:30–10:4

Questions for Interaction

Leader
Refer to the Summary and Study Notes at the end of this session as needed. If 30 minutes is not enough time to answer all of the questions in this section, conclude the Bible Study by answering question 7.

1. What would you say is the general view in your community about how a person can get to heaven?

   ○ By being moral and doing good deeds.
   ○ By going to church.
   ○ By believing in Jesus.
   ○ Most of my neighbors don't believe in heaven.
   ○ Other _____.

2. Who was Israel's "stumbling stone" (9:32)? Where do people you interact with stumble when it comes to accepting Jesus?

3. What hope does Paul have for the Israelites in the first verse of chapter 10?

4. Why did Israel's belief in doing enough righteous deeds to get into heaven not work?

5. What is the distinguishing difference between a "way of works" to gain righteous standing before God versus a "way of faith"?

6. Do you know religious people who have great zeal but do not accept Jesus? How does that make you feel?

7. Whose eternal destiny are you most concerned about? How can you help them get over their "stumbling stone" so they can come to know and accept Jesus?

Going Deeper   If your group has time and/or wants a challenge, go on to this question.

8. What does it mean that Christ is the "end of the law" (10:4)? How does this support Paul's argument that the way to heaven is through faith and not works?

Caring Time Apply the Lesson and Pray for One Another (15 minutes)

Once again, take some time now to encourage one another in your faith by discussing the following questions and sharing prayer requests.

1. Where are you in the journey of following Christ?

   ○ I am a seeker.
   ○ I have just begun the journey.
   ○ I'm returning after getting lost on the wrong path.
   ○ I've been following Christ for a long time.
   ○ Other _____.

2. How are you doing at inviting people to fill "the empty chair"?

3. How would you like the group to pray for the person(s) you mentioned in question #7?

> **Leader**
> Be sure to save at least 15 minutes for this important time. After sharing responses to all three questions and asking for prayer requests, close in a time of group prayer.

NEXT WEEK *Today we looked at Israel's unbelief and rejection of Jesus. We saw how Jesus became a "stumbling stone" for them, because they wanted to believe in their own good works instead of God's grace. In the coming week, look for opportunities to share the love of Jesus with others and pray zealously for their souls. Next week, we will look at how God has made salvation available to everyone.*

Summary: The failure of the Jews was not only a part of God's plan (Rom. 9:6–26), but it was also a matter of their own choice. Paul shows this by contrasting two ways of relating to God. One was the way of works. The Jews meticulously kept the Law so as to build up a credit balance of righteousness (thus putting God in one's debt and earning his friendship). Of course, this never worked because of human sinfulness. The other was the way of faith. Rather, being suddenly and unexpectedly confronted with his love as exhibited in Christ, the Gentiles responded in trusting obedience. The way of faith is contrasted with the way of works.

9:32 *pursue.* The problem was not that Israel pursued righteousness, but that they did so by works and not by faith. The contrast is between righteousness sought through deeds, and righteousness that is not sought at all but simply accepted by faith. *the stumbling stone.* In Matthew 21:42, Jesus identifies himself as "the stone that the builders rejected" (quoting Psalm 118:22–23). Thus, the early Christian church came to recognize that the somewhat mysterious references to a stone in the Old Testament refer to Jesus. The idea of Christ as the stone occurs at various points in the New Testament as well (Acts 4:11; Eph. 2:20; 1 Peter 2:4–8). In not recognizing Jesus as the inner meaning of the Law, Israel can do little else than stumble over him.

9:33 Paul weaves together two passages from Isaiah to show that the failure of Israel to believe in Christ had been foretold by Old Testament Scriptures. *stumble.* As in a race, a runner cannot win if he trips over a large stone. In this case, that very stone is he who brings salvation to those who trust him by faith.

10:1 The fact that Paul continues to pray for the salvation of Israel is a clear indication that he does not consider their rejection as final and complete.

10:2 *zeal.* In ancient times, the Jews were noted for their fanatical and fervent religious zeal. They were desperately earnest about keeping the Law, even when it involved great personal sacrifices or danger: e.g., Eleazar, the priest, allowed himself to be whipped to death rather than to eat pork, as ordered by the Syrian king, Antiochus Epiphanes. *not according to knowledge.* This is the flaw in their zeal. They fail to know God as he really is, as he is revealed in Jesus Christ.

10:3 Paul describes the precise nature of Israel's blindness: they did not see that the status of righteousness is a gift that "comes from God." Instead, they insisted that it was through their own good deeds that righteousness was established.

10:4 *Christ is the end of the law.* It is not completely clear what Paul means here. He may mean this in the sense that obedience to the Law is no longer the way by which people are accepted by God. Or he may mean that Christ is the "goal" of the Law, i.e., Christ is the sort of person the Law speaks about.

Salvation Is for Everyone

Scripture Romans 10:5–21

Ice-Breaker Connect With Your Group (15 minutes)

In today's Scripture passage, we will see how God judges our faith by what we believe in our hearts and confess with our mouths. Take turns sharing times in your life when you had to judge or be judged.

Leader
To help new group members get acquainted, remember to do all three Ice-Breaker questions.

1. Have you or has someone you know served on a jury? What was it like (or what do you think it would be like) having to decide whether someone was guilty or innocent?

   ○ Chilling.
   ○ Rewarding.
   ○ Painful.
   ○ Fun.
   ○ Other _____.

2. What should you have gotten in trouble for as a kid but got away with it? How guilty did you feel?

   ○ Stealing.
   ○ Skipping school.
   ○ Speeding.
   ○ Dating someone my parents disapproved of.
   ○ Cheating on a test.
   ○ Other _____.

3. Was there a time when you received mercy from your parents instead of being disciplined? What was it for?

 Bible Study Read Scripture and Discuss (30 minutes)

Paul continues to contrast the way of works with the way of faith. The way of works, which the Jews attempted to follow, does not lead to God because we are all sinful. The way of faith depends on God's grace and leads to eternal life. This way is quite simple, but the results are life changing. Read Romans 10:5–21 and note how God reaches out to everyone.

Salvation Is for Everyone

[5]For Moses writes about the righteousness that is from the law: The one who does these things will live by them. [6]But the righteousness that comes from faith speaks like this: Do not say in your heart, "Who will go up to heaven?" that is, to bring Christ down [7]or, "Who will go down into the abyss?" that is, to bring Christ up from the dead. [8]On the contrary, what does it say? The message is near you, in your mouth and in your heart. This is the message of faith that we proclaim: [9]if you confess with your mouth, "Jesus is Lord," and believe in your heart that God raised Him from the dead, you will be saved. [10]With the heart one believes, resulting in righteousness, and with the mouth one confesses, resulting in salvation. [11]Now the Scripture says, No one who believes on Him will be put to shame, [12]for there is no distinction between Jew and Greek, since the same Lord of all is rich to all who call on Him. [13]For everyone who calls on the name of the Lord will be saved.

[14]But how can they call on Him in whom they have not believed? And how can they believe without hearing about Him? And how can they hear without a preacher? [15]And how can they preach unless they are sent? As it is written: How welcome are the feet of those who announce the gospel of good things! [16]But all did not obey the gospel. For Isaiah says, Lord, who has believed our message? [17]So faith comes from what is heard, and what is heard comes through the message about Christ. [18]But I ask, "Did they not hear?" Yes, they did:

Their voice has gone out to all the earth,
and their words to the ends of the inhabited world.

[19]But I ask, "Did Israel not understand?" First, Moses said:

I will make you jealous of those who are not a nation;
I will make you angry by a nation that lacks understanding.

[20]And Isaiah says boldly:

I was found by those who were not looking for Me;
I revealed Myself to those who were not asking for Me.

[21]But to Israel he says: All day long I have spread out My hands to a disobedient and defiant people.

Romans 10:5–21

Questions for Interaction

Leader
Refer to the Summary and Study Notes at the end of this session as needed. If 30 minutes is not enough time to answer all of the questions in this section, conclude the Bible Study by answering question 7.

1. When do you have trouble believing what someone is telling you?

   ○ When a solicitor calls me trying to sell me something.
   ○ When I watch infomercials on TV.
   ○ When my teenager comes in late and has an excuse.
   ○ When I'm buying a used car.
   ○ Other _____.

2. What are the two main contentions Israel has with God about salvation? How could Israel reject Jesus when they knew about his coming through prophecy?

3. According to verses 9 and 10, how is one saved? How important is our inner and external response?

4. What does it mean to confess "Jesus is Lord"? How does this tie in with belief?

5. How does God get the salvation message to people (vv. 14–15)? What is our part in delivering that message?

6. What do you see as the basic difference between Christianity and other religions?

7. When did you understand that the message of Christ applied to you personally? How did that realization change your life?

Going Deeper   If your group has time and/or wants a challenge, go on to this question.

---

8. According to verses 16–21, did Israel have every chance to hear the message? Can the same be said of all people in the world today?

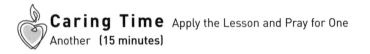

Caring Time
Apply the Lesson and Pray for One Another (15 minutes)

Keeping in mind that "everyone who calls on the name of the Lord will be saved" (v. 13), gather around each other now in a time of sharing and prayer. Begin by sharing your responses to the following questions.

1. What's the immediate forecast for the "weather" in your life?

   ○ Sunny and warm.
   ○ Overcast.
   ○ Chance for showers.
   ○ Partly cloudy.
   ○ Other _____.

2. Who first shared the "gospel of good things" (v. 15) with you? What would you say to that person if he or she walked into the room?

3. How can you bring the "gospel of good things" into the life of a particular friend or family member this coming week?

NEXT WEEK *Today we were reminded once again of how God has made salvation available to everyone through the way of faith and not the way of works. We saw that the way of faith involves both our hearts and mouths. We must believe in our hearts that "Jesus is Lord," and then make it known publicly by confessing it with our mouths to others. In the coming week, follow through on sharing the Good News with the person you mentioned in answer to question #3 in the Caring Time. Next week we will focus on the mercy God has poured out on Israel and how we, also, are recipients of that mercy.*

Leader
Encourage everyone to participate in this important time and be sure that each group member is receiving prayer support. Continue to pray for the empty chair in the closing group prayer.

Summary: Paul has revealed to his readers the way of faith. Now he explains the benefits of faith and how we come to faith. The Jews had depended upon obedience to the Law for right standing before God. Paul announces that righteousness comes from faith. Everyone no matter what background they have or how good they have been must come before God in faith to be saved.

10:6 *Do not say in your heart.* These are the opening words in the Greek translation of Deuteronomy 8:17 and 9:4—both of which warn against boasting of one's own accomplishments. *Who will go up to heaven?* This phrase means that Israel does not have to go all the way up to heaven (where God lives) to find God's Law (Deut. 30:12). *that is.* Three times (in vv. 6–8) this phrase is used to indicate that what follows is Paul's interpretation of the preceding phrase. This is typical rabbinical exegesis. *to bring Christ down.* The passage found in Deuteronomy refers to the Law, but since Paul sees Christ as the fulfillment of the Law (v. 4), it is legitimate for him to apply this phrase to Christ. Just as it was not necessary to scale heaven to get to the Law, neither was it necessary to go there and bring down Christ. He has already come to earth. Both the Law and the incarnate Christ are gifts of God to human beings.

10:7 *abyss.* The depths of the earth or the place of the dead—Sheol. This word was also used to describe the depths of the sea (Gen. 1:2), hence Paul's translation here of Deuteronomy 30:13. *bring Christ up.* Nor is there any need to bring Christ up from the dead, since he has already been raised.

10:8 Just as the Law did not have to be sought vigorously, neither does Christ. Both the Law and the one to whom it points are near and are to be affirmed verbally and received graciously. *message of faith.* Paul boldly identifies the "word" in Deuteronomy 30:14 with the Gospel message—since Christ is himself the fulfiller of the Law and the inner meaning of the Law (vv. 4–5).

10:9 *confess with your mouth/believe in your heart.* Paul applies the quote of verse 8 to Christ. The "message of faith" (v. 8) that is to fill the mouth and heart of a Christian is the central Christian confession of Christ's lordship and resurrection. To be a Christian involves not only inner belief but also outer witness to that belief. It is to declare publicly on whose side one stands. *Lord.* Jesus is to be Lord, in contrast to the Roman emperor (to whom this title was normally given). "Lord" was also used some 6,000 times in the Greek Old Testament as the name of God. To call Jesus Lord is to give him both worship and obedience. *raised Him from the dead.* This is the distinctive confession of the Christian. In rising from the dead, Jesus verified his claim to be Lord. *saved.* To be saved is to be granted eternal life; i.e., to share the life of God both here and now, and fully in the future when Christ returns.

10:10 Belief is said to issue in justification, and confession in salvation. In fact, justification and salvation are synonymous here (see v. 9), where salvation is said to be the product of these two realities. *heart.* In Jewish thought, the heart was considered to be the center of the person; the site of one's intellect, emotion and will. *confesses.* Notice that in verse 9 confession is first and belief is second. (Paul is probably following the order in Deuteronomy 30:14.) Here the more natural order is found: first you believe, then you confess.

10:12 *no distinction.* In Romans 3:23, the emphasis is negative: all are sinners. Here the emphasis is positive: all can be saved by faith. *the same Lord.* The God of the Jews is the God of the Gentiles—an amazing thought in the days when Paul wrote.

10:14–15 *they.* Paul repeats this word over and over again. The "they" he refers to is Israel (in particular) and all men and women (in general).

10:15 *preach.* The word means to proclaim like a herald. The related word, proclamation, came to mean "the Gospel message" (Rom. 16:25–26).

10:18 This is a literal quotation from the Greek version of Psalm 19:4. The spread of the Gospel was amazing as Justin Martyr, writing in the mid-second century, states: "There is no people, Greek or barbarian, or of any other race, by whatever appellation or manners they may be distinguished, however ignorant of arts or agriculture, whether they dwell in tents or wander about in covered wagons, among whom prayers and thanksgivings are not offered in the name of the crucified Jesus to the Father and Creator of all things."

God's Mercy Is for Everyone

Scripture Romans 11:1–26

LAST WEEK *In last week's session, we continued to look at how God has made salvation available to everyone through the way of faith and not the way of works. We were reminded that God's way is simple; all we have to do is believe in our hearts that God raised Jesus from the dead and confess with our mouths "Jesus is Lord." Today we will look at how God's mercy is given to everyone, including Israel, so that all can come to repentance.*

 Ice-Breaker Connect With Your Group (15 minutes)

Sharing is something that we were all taught to do as children, but often struggle with, even as adults. The Jews found it difficult to share God with the Gentiles. Take turns sharing some of your thoughts and experiences with sharing.

Leader
Choose one or two of the Ice-Breaker questions. If you have a new group member you may want to do all three. Remember to stick closely to the three-part agenda and the time allowed for each segment.

1. As a child, what did you have the most difficulty sharing with others?

   ○ My toys.
   ○ My candy.
   ○ My bike.
   ○ My friendship.
   ○ Other _____.

2. As an adult, what do you have the most difficulty sharing with others?

   ○ The remote control.
   ○ My time.
   ○ My money.
   ○ My faith.
   ○ Other _____.

3. What experience that you've had in life would you like to be able to share with others in this group?

Bible Study Read Scripture and Discuss (30 minutes)

In the following passage, Paul explains how Israel's rejection of Jesus was the Gentiles opportunity to receive the mercy of God and connect with Jesus. Does God then reject Israel for rejecting himself? Read Romans 11:1–26 and note how Paul answers that question.

Leader
Ask two members of the group, selected ahead of time, to read aloud the Scripture passage. Have one person read verses 1–10; the second person read verses 11–26. Then discuss the Questions for Interaction, dividing into subgroups of three to six.

God's Mercy Is for Everyone

Reader 1:   11 I ask, then, has God rejected His people? Absolutely not! For I too am an Israelite, a descendant of Abraham, from the tribe of Benjamin. ²God has not rejected His people whom He foreknew. Or do you not know what the Scripture says in the Elijah section—how he pleads with God against Israel?

³Lord, they have killed Your prophets, torn down Your altars; and I am the only one left, and they are trying to take my life! ⁴But what was God's reply to him? I have left 7,000 men for Myself who have not bowed down to Baal. ⁵In the same way, then, there is also at the present time a remnant chosen by grace. ⁶Now if by grace, then it is not by works; otherwise grace ceases to be grace.

⁷What then? Israel did not find what it was looking for, but the elect did find it. The rest were hardened, ⁸as it is written:

God gave them a spirit of stupor,
eyes that cannot see and ears that cannot hear, to this day.

⁹And David says:

Let their feasting become a snare and a trap,
a pitfall and a retribution to them.
¹⁰Let their eyes be darkened so they cannot see,
and their backs be bent continually.

Reader 2:   ¹¹I ask, then, have they stumbled so as to fall? Absolutely not! On the contrary, by their stumbling, salvation has come to the Gentiles to make Israel jealous. ¹²Now if their stumbling brings riches for the world, and their failure riches for the Gentiles, how much more will their full number bring! ¹³Now I am speaking to you Gentiles. In view of the fact that I am an apostle to the Gentiles, I magnify my ministry, ¹⁴if I can somehow make my own people jealous and save some of them. ¹⁵For if their being rejected is world reconciliation, what will their acceptance mean but life from the dead?

¹⁶Now if the firstfruits offered up are holy, so is the whole batch. And if the root is holy, so are the branches. ¹⁷Now if some of the branches were broken off, and you, though a wild olive branch, were grafted in among them, and have come to share in the

rich root of the cultivated olive tree, [18]do not brag that you are better than those branches. But if you do brag—you do not sustain the root, but the root sustains you. [19]Then you will say, "Branches were broken off so that I might be grafted in." [20]True enough; they were broken off by unbelief, but you stand by faith. Do not be arrogant, but be afraid. [21]For if God did not spare the natural branches, He will not spare you either.

[22]Therefore, consider God's kindness and severity: severity toward those who have fallen, but God's kindness toward you—if you remain in His kindness. Otherwise you too will be cut off. [23]And even they, if they do not remain in unbelief, will be grafted in, because God has the power to graft them in again. [24]For if you were cut off from your native wild olive, and against nature were grafted into a cultivated olive tree, how much more will these—the natural branches—be grafted into their own olive tree?

[25]So that you will not be conceited, brothers, I do not want you to be unaware of this secret: a partial hardening has come to Israel until the full number of the Gentiles has come in. [26]And in this way all Israel will be saved.

Romans 11:1–26

Questions for Interaction

Leader
Refer to the Summary and Study Notes at the end of this session as needed. If 30 minutes is not enough time to answer all of the questions in this section, conclude the Bible Study by answering question 7.

1. When have you felt like you were really accepted and part of a group?

   ○ With my best friends in high school.
   ○ With a sorority/fraternity.
   ○ With a sports team.
   ○ With this group!
   ○ Other _____.

2. Who is the "remnant chosen by grace" in verse 5? What does it mean to be chosen by grace?

3. What does it mean to be "hardened" (vv. 7–8)? Is that something Israel did? God did? Or both? What was the result of Israel's hardening (v. 11)?

4. Why did Paul tell the Gentiles to be afraid in verse 20? Why would God not spare the Gentiles (v. 22)?

5. Does Paul mean in verses 25–26 that every Jewish person will ultimately be saved? Why or why not?

6. How do you struggle with works versus grace? In what ways are works still important?

7. When have you experienced God's mercy? In what way do you need God's mercy right now?

8. What should be America's relationship with Israel in light of the teaching of chapters 9–11? Should it be any different than with a country of another religion? Why or why not?

Caring Time   Apply the Lesson and Pray for One Another   (15 minutes)

Knowing that God is merciful and forgiving, come before him now in this time of sharing and prayer. Encourage and support one another so you don't become "hardened" to God's goodness and grace.

Leader
Be sure to save at least 15 minutes for this time of prayer and encouragement. Continue to encourage group members to invite new people to the group.

1. What season are you experiencing in your spiritual life right now?

   ❍ The warmth of summer.
   ❍ The dead of winter.
   ❍ The new life of spring.
   ❍ The changes of fall.

2. What world events are especially worrying you right now? Include prayer for peace in Jerusalem and all of the Middle East.

3. Pray for the concerns mentioned by each group member when answering question 7 regarding the need for God's mercy.

NEXT WEEK *Today we looked at how the mercy of God has been made available not only to Israel but to the whole world. All a person has to do is accept that mercy and experience God's grace. In the coming week, adopt a missionary that you will pray for and support as he or she tries to reach out to foreigners with this Good News of God's mercy. Next week we will consider what it means to devote ourselves to God as his followers.*

Summary: The theme of chapter 11 is stated in verse 2a, "God has not rejected His people whom he foreknew." Paul begins by pointing out that a remnant of Jewish believers already exists (vv. 1–10). Then, looking at the unbelieving majority, he asserts that their exclusion will not last forever (vv. 11–24).

11:1 *I too am an Israelite.* Paul himself—a true Jew who is also a believing Christian—is proof that God has not cast off Israel and is still using Israel (through Paul) to fulfill its God-given task of bearing God's message to the world. In other words, God is still working through Israel, so he cannot have cast them off.

11:2–5 Even in Elijah's day, those who remained faithful did so by God's grace. Because this remnant was of grace and not of works, its existence brings hope to the unfaithful majority that God has not abandoned Israel. So in Paul's day, the small band of believing Jews is also a guarantee of the continuing election of the whole of Israel.

11:4 *7,000.* It has been suggested that not only is this the estimate of the number of those who remained faithful during a time of apostasy, but also it is a number which served as a symbol of perfection or completeness (seven and multiples thereof have that significance in Judaism). So here God is declaring that he will bring to completion his plan of salvation for Israel.

11:5 *remnant.* The prophets, especially, saw that at no time was all of Israel faithful to God. On the other hand, there was always at least a small number who were true. They were like a nation within a nation. So when speaking of "the chosen people," Paul was thinking of that minority.

11:7 *hardened.* A Greek word used to describe a kidney stone or callous, which came to be used metaphorically—a heart hardens like a stone into insensitivity. As Paul will soon show, this hardening is not God's last word.

11:8 *spirit of stupor.* This phrase, as used in Isaiah 29:10, describes a "state of spiritual insensitivity."

11:9 *their feasting/a snare.* However this image is intended to be understood—as a cloth spread for a meal entangling the feet (as those eating spring up to ward off sudden danger), or as poisoned food which they are forced to eat—the root idea is that the very security of those feasting peacefully is the source of their ruin. So Israel, resting peacefully in her calling as God's "chosen people," fails to note her own faithlessness and hardening, thinking herself beyond reproach.

11:14 *jealous.* Envy is usually something that is negative. In this case it brings good to pass. *save.* Convert them to the Christian faith. *some of them.* While he is confident that in the end "all Israel will be saved" (v. 26), for the moment his hopes are somewhat limited.

11:15 The rejection by the Jews means that the Gospel is being preached to the rest of the world with success.

11:16 *firstfruits.* An Old Testament image (Num. 15:17–21). The first grains harvested were ground, baked and then presented as an offering to God. Thereafter, the rest of the grain would be counted as holy or sacred.

root/branches. A second picture follows from the first. In like fashion, the root (i.e., the patriarchs) was sacred to God. So, too, was the nation holy (or set apart to God).

11:17 *branches were broken off.* In terms of the metaphor, Paul is referring here to unbelieving Israel. *a wild olive branch.* The Gentile Christians. *among them.* The remaining branches; i.e., the Jewish Christians.

11:18–22 A strong warning to Gentile Christians not to despise the Jews.

11:23 God has the power to graft Israel back into the olive tree. Christians ought to wait in expectation for this miracle.

11:25 *secret.* In contrast to the contemporary use of this word and its emphasis on secrecy and hiddeness, a mystery in the New Testament is something which was hidden in the mind of God, but which now he is pleased to reveal to all. It is something a person could never have figured out alone, but once disclosed it is to be proclaimed to all who will hear (i.e., not kept hidden). *hardening.* The nature of the hardening is not clear. It was not just a matter of human disobedience (although that was involved), but it was of God. It was only in part (there was always a remnant). It was temporary (until the fullness of the Gentiles came into the kingdom), and it was for the benefit of the Gentiles. *full number.* The full number of the elect of the Gentiles.

11:26 *all Israel will be saved.* Here Paul is affirming what he longs for—the salvation of all of Israel over against what he then knew: only a remnant of believers.

Devoted Followers

Scripture Romans 12:1–21

LAST WEEK *God's faithful mercy was our topic for discussion in last week's session. We saw how God has mercy on everyone, including Israel, so that all can come to repentance. Today, Paul will remind us how we, as followers of Christ, should live out our faith and demonstrate our devotion to God. We will also see how love is always to be the guiding factor in our relationships with others, Christians and non-Christians alike.*

Ice-Breaker Connect With Your Group (15 minutes)

There are pressures all around us that encourage us to conform to the world's lifestyle and way of thinking. Take turns sharing how you handle these pressures in your life.

1. As a teenager, how did peer pressure affect the way you dressed? How about your hairstyle?

2. What is your favorite movie of all time? What did you learn from it?

3. Who do you turn to for advice when making decisions?

- ○ Your spouse.
- ○ A brother or sister.
- ○ Your parents.
- ○ Your best friend.
- ○ A coworker you greatly respect.
- ○ Your pastor.
- ○ A group member.
- ○ Your boss.
- ○ No one.
- ○ Other _____.

Leader

Introduce and welcome group members. If there are no new members, choose one or two of the Ice-Breaker questions to get started. If there are new members, then discuss all three.

Bible Study Read Scripture and Discuss (30 minutes)

In today's passage, Paul teaches the Romans, and us, that being devoted to Christ requires behavior change. However, we cannot change on our own. We need God's help. Read Romans 12:1–21 and note three things we can do to develop our relationship with God. Also, note several behaviors that should be demonstrated in our lives as a result of this spiritual work.

Leader
Select a member of the group ahead of time to read aloud the Scripture passage. Then discuss the Questions for Interaction, dividing into subgroups of three to six.

Devoted Followers

12 Therefore, brothers, by the mercies of God, I urge you to present your bodies as a living sacrifice, holy and pleasing to God; this is your spiritual worship. [2]Do not be conformed to this age, but be transformed by the renewing of your mind, so that you may discern what is the good, pleasing, and perfect will of God.

[3]For by the grace given to me, I tell everyone among you not to think of himself more highly than he should think. Instead, think sensibly, as God has distributed a measure of faith to each one. [4]Now as we have many parts in one body, and all the parts do not have the same function, [5]in the same way we who are many are one body in Christ and individually members of one another. [6]According to the grace given to us, we have different gifts:

If prophecy, use it according to the standard of faith;
[7]if service, in service; if teaching, in teaching;
[8]if exhorting, in exhortation; giving, with generosity;
leading, with diligence; showing mercy, with cheerfulness.

[9]Love must be without hypocrisy. Detest evil; cling to what is good. [10]Show family affection to one another with brotherly love. Outdo one another in showing honor. [11]Do not lack diligence; be fervent in spirit; serve the Lord. [12]Rejoice in hope; be patient in affliction; be persistent in prayer. [13]Share with the saints in their needs; pursue hospitality. [14]Bless those who persecute you; bless and do not curse. [15]Rejoice with those who rejoice; weep with those who weep. [16]Be in agreement with one another. Do not be proud; instead, associate with the humble. Do not be wise in your own estimation. [17]Do not repay anyone evil for evil. Try to do what is honorable in everyone's eyes. [18]If possible, on your part, live at peace with everyone. [19]Friends, do not avenge yourselves; instead, leave room for His wrath. For it is written: Vengeance belongs to Me; I will repay, says the Lord. [20]But

If your enemy is hungry, feed him.
If he is thirsty, give him something to drink.
For in so doing you will be heaping fiery coals on his head.
[21]Do not be conquered by evil, but conquer evil with good.

Romans 12:1–21

Questions for Interaction

Leader
Refer to the Summary and Study Notes at the end of this session as needed. If 30 minutes is not enough time to answer all of the questions in this section, conclude the Bible Study by answering question 7.

1. What do you think is the hardest thing about being a follower of Christ?

   ○ Having a lot of rules to live by.
   ○ Being persecuted because of my faith.
   ○ Sharing my faith with others.
   ○ Loving everyone, no matter what they do to me.
   ○ Other _____.

2. What does it mean to "present your bodies as a living sacrifice" (v. 1)?

3. What does Paul mean, "do not be conformed to this age" (v. 2)? What are some examples of this? How does the renewing of your mind happen?

4. Are you more likely to over estimate or to under estimate your spiritual gifts? Of the six gifts listed here, where are you the strongest?

5. Look at the characteristics and behaviors of a Christian in verses 9–21. Which one is hardest for you? Which one is easiest?

6. How can you acquire the character trait that is hardest for you? How can being a living sacrifice, not conforming to this age and renewing your mind help you?

7. In what current situation do you need to know God's will, instead of conforming to what the world would want you to do?

Going Deeper   If your group has time and/or wants a challenge, go on to this question.

8. What does Paul mean in verse 20 when he says that showing kindness to our enemy will heap "fiery coals on his head"? What is our part in conquering evil with good?

Caring Time
Apply the Lesson and Pray for One Another (15 minutes)

Take some time now to "rejoice with those who rejoice" and "weep with those who weep." Begin by sharing your answers to the following questions. Then share prayer requests and close with prayer.

1. What was the high point of last week for you? What was the low point?

2. What one behavior listed in verses 9–21 do you need us to pray with you about developing?

3. How can the group help you to become a more devoted follower of Christ?

Leader
Continue to encourage group members to invite new people to the group. Remind everyone that this group is for learning and sharing, but also for reaching out to others. Close the group prayer by thanking God for each member and for this time together.

NEXT WEEK *Today we looked at how we should live out our faith and devote ourselves to God. We were reminded that this doesn't just happen, but it requires some effort on our part. We must apply ourselves to three key principles: yielding to the Holy Spirit, resisting worldly influences and renewing our minds with God's truth. In the coming week, devote more time to prayer and less time to TV or other worldly influences. Next week we will look at the believer's responsibility to government authorities.*

Summary: From doctrine Paul now turns, almost by reflex, to duty: how one lives flows quite naturally out of what one believes. The issue of the Christian lifestyle has never been far from Paul's mind. It is there in his description of the pervasiveness of sin (1:18–3:20, especially 3:8). It surfaces explicitly in chapter 6: How can you go on sinning if you have been baptized into Christ's death? A person serves one master or another—God or sin. In chapters 7 and 8 the difficulty of overturning sin's tyranny is Paul's focus. Now in the next three chapters, Paul spells out in concrete and particular terms what he has previously expressed abstractly and generally.

In verses 3–8, Paul turns to the Christian community as a whole—understanding it to be composed of believers with different gifts. Paul concludes his brief discussion of spiritual gifts with emphasis on the fact that whatever gift one has, it should be exercised with enthusiasm for the good of others. Paul then offers a series of loosely connected exhortations by way of further explanation of verses 1 and 2, focused first on relationships between Christians (vv. 9–13) and then on relationships with those outside the church (vv. 14–21).

12:1 *Therefore.* Christian ethics emerge out of Christian theology; Christian obedience is a response to Christian truth. *by the mercies of God.* Paul has just declared God's amazing mercy in chapter 11. A Christian's motivation to obedience is overwhelming gratitude for God's mercy. *sacrifice.* In the Old Testament sacrificial system, the victim of the sacrifice becomes wholly the property of God. The sacrifice becomes holy, i.e., set apart for God only. *spiritual worship.* Paul may mean by this an inner movement on the part of a person toward God (in contrast to external rites). But since the word translated "spiritual" can be rendered "rational," the idea may be that believers render intelligent worship. This meaning is given credence by the emphasis in verse 2.

12:2 *Do not be conformed.* Literally, "stop allowing yourself to be conformed"; i.e., believers are no longer helpless victims of natural and supernatural forces that would shape them into a distorted pattern; rather they now have the ability and help to resist such powers. *be transformed.* The force of the verb is "continue to let yourself be transformed"; i.e., a continuous action by the Holy Spirit that goes on for a lifetime. A Christian's responsibility is to stay open

to this sanctification process as the Spirit works to teach him or her to look at life from God's view of reality. *renewing of your mind.* Develop a spiritual sensitivity and perception—learn to look at life on the basis of God's view of reality. Paul emphasizes the need to develop understanding of God's ways.

12:3 *measure of faith.* Believers are not to measure themselves against others, but rather to evaluate themselves by how well they are living in accord with how God desires people to live.

12:5 *members of one another.* This is the critical insight that makes for harmony in the church. Believers must recognize that they are interdependent, needing to give to and receive from one another.

12:9 *Love. Agape:* self-giving action on behalf of others made possible by God's Spirit. Thus far in Romans when Paul spoke of love, it was in reference to God's love (1:7; 5:5,8; 8:35,37,39; 9:13,25; 11:28). There is one exception to this, namely 8:28, where he speaks of a person's love for God. But here in verse 9 the focus shifts. Paul's concern is how the Christian relates to other people. This becomes especially clear in

13:8–10 *without hypocrisy.* Genuine, not counterfeit or showy. It is possible to pretend (even to one's self) to love others.

12:10 *brotherly love.* A second word for love is used here, *philadelphia*, denoting the tender affection found in families, now said to be appropriate to those in the church—which is the Christian's new family.

12:11 *fervent.* This Greek word is also used of water that is boiling (or of metal, like copper, which is glowing red-hot).

12:12 What makes it possible to endure affliction is joyful hope in one's inheritance in the age to come, coupled with daily, continuous prayer.

12:13 To be "renewed" (v. 2) is not just an interior matter of mind and emotions, but involves concrete outer action such as giving to those in need.

12:15 Believers demonstrate love to nonbelievers by being sensitive and responsive to their joys and sorrows.

12:16 Christians ought to provide a model of harmony for the world around them. Avoiding haughtiness, they ought to put in its place unselfconscious association with all types of people.

12:17 *Do not repay anyone evil for evil.* A common Christian teaching (1 Thess. 5:15; 1 Peter 3:9). Christians are called upon to do not just what the consensus calls "good," but those things that are inherently "good." These deeds will be recognized as such by those of good will.

12:18 *live at peace.* This is the normative principle in these verses. Christians are to work at creating harmonious relationships with all.

12:19–20 Seeking peace means doing away with the principle of revenge and the continual escalation of violence. Using quotes from Deuteronomy 32:35 and Proverbs 25:21–22, Paul reminds Christians that they are to leave judgment to God while they do all in their power to turn an enemy into a friend.

12:20 *fiery coals.* Providing kindness of every sort to one's enemies may induce the kind of inner shame that leads to repentance, and hence to reconciliation and true friendship.

12:21 People who retaliate have allowed evil to overcome them. They have given in to their evil desires and have become like their enemies.

Submission to Authorities

Scripture Romans 13:1–7

LAST WEEK *Last week Paul encouraged us to "not be conformed ... but be transformed" (12:2). We were reminded how we, as followers of Christ, should live out our faith and demonstrate our devotion to God. We also saw how love is our guide to relationships with others, whether they are fellow believers or not. Today we will turn our attention to the responsibility that Christians have toward government authorities.*

Ice-Breaker Connect With Your Group (15 minutes)

Bringing up politics is a great way to get some lively dinner conversation going! Our daily lives are impacted by government policies and regulations. Some we agree with and some we don't. Take turns sharing some of your thoughts about politics and government.

Leader
Choose one, two or all three of the Ice-Breaker questions. Be sure to welcome and introduce new group members.

1. If you were asked to be a politician, what office would you want? Why?

   ○ President.
   ○ State Senator or Representative.
   ○ U.S. Senator or Representative.
   ○ Mayor.
   ○ Governor.
   ○ School Board Representative.
   ○ Sheriff.
   ○ Judge.
   ○ Dog Catcher.
   ○ Other _____.

2. If you could change any existing law, what would it be?

   ○ Allowing smoking in public buildings.
   ○ Limiting smoking in public buildings.
   ○ Change the speed limit on interstate highways.
   ○ Allow for the medical use of marijuana.
   ○ Raise the minimum age of drivers.
   ○ Lower the minimum age of drivers.
   ○ Raise the gas tax.
   ○ Lower the gas tax.
   ○ Add more environmental protection.
   ○ Decrease environmental protection.
   ○ Eliminate local zoning ordinances.
   ○ Other _____.

3. If you could add a new law, what would it be?

Bible Study Read Scripture and Discuss (30 minutes)

God has created order in society by establishing authorities and governmental principles by which nations are to be led. Paul teaches that Christians have a duty and responsibility in society to be model citizens. Read Romans 13:1–7 and note what those responsibilities are in relation to government authorities.

Leader
Select two members of the group ahead of time to read aloud the Scripture passage. Then discuss the Questions for Interaction, dividing into subgroups of three to six.

Submission to Authorities

Reader One: 13 Everyone must submit to the governing authorities, for there is no authority except from God, and those that exist are instituted by God. [2]So then, the one who resists the authority is opposing God's command,

Reader Two: and those who oppose it will bring judgment on themselves.

Reader One: [3]For rulers are not a terror to good conduct,

Reader Two: but to bad. Do you want to be unafraid of the authority?

Reader One: Do good and you will have its approval. [4]For government is God's servant to you for good.

Reader Two: But if you do wrong, be afraid, because it does not carry the sword for no reason. For government is God's servant, an avenger that brings wrath on the one who does wrong. [5]Therefore, you must submit, not only because of wrath, but also because of your conscience.

Reader One: [6]And for this reason you pay taxes, since the authorities are God's public servants, continually attending to these tasks. [7]Pay your obligations to everyone: taxes to those you owe taxes, tolls to those you owe tolls, respect to those you owe respect, and honor to those you owe honor.

Romans 13:1-7

Questions for Interaction

Leader
Refer to the Summary and Study Notes at the end of this session as needed. If 30 minutes is not enough time to answer all of the questions in this section, conclude the Bible Study by answering question 7.

1. How do you feel about the taxes withheld from your paycheck?

   ○ The politicians just waste the money.
   ○ It would be all right if everyone carried the same tax burden.
   ○ I would like more say in how my tax dollars are spent.
   ○ The money should be given to local government.
   ○ The federal government should control all the spending.
   ○ It is unfair that the people that are the most productive pay the most.
   ○ It is unfair that the people that can't afford to pay taxes carry such a burden.
   ○ Other _____.

2. Why do you think a conversation involving religion and politics is difficult for some people to have?

3. Why does Paul say we should submit to governing authorities? When is it okay not to submit to these authorities?

4. How have recent terror events changed the way we view the government's responsibility to be "God's servants"? What should we do if we don't like how a government leader is handling his or her duties?

5. What do you struggle with regarding submitting to authority?

   ○ Respecting politicians.
   ○ Paying certain taxes.
   ○ Respecting my employer's management decisions.
   ○ Respecting my parents.
   ○ Respecting church leaders.
   ○ Other _____.

6. How could you improve on how you relate to the authorities in your life?

7. How well are you submitting to God's authority and his will for your life right now? How could you improve?

8. What are Christians to do if they believe governing authorities are wicked and breaking God's law? What's the difference between submitting to authorities and unconditionally obeying them?

Caring Time Apply the Lesson and Pray for One Another (15 minutes)

Leader
Have you started working with your group about their mission—perhaps by sharing the dream of multiplying into two groups by the end of this study of Romans?

With all of the uncertainty and political unrest in the world, it helps to have the support and encouragement of other Christians. Gather around each other now for a time of sharing and prayer.

1. How was your walk with the Lord this past week?

2. Let's pray today for:

   ○ The president of the United States.
   ○ Other national leaders.
   ○ Our military men and women.
   ○ State and local leaders.
   ○ Other _____.

3. Let's also pray for the people in our nation. Pray that God would bless America and that Americans would be open to hearing the good news of Jesus. Ask for boldness in sharing the Gospel.

NEXT WEEK *Today we looked at the believer's responsibility to government authorities. We were reminded to be respectful of those authorities and pray for them. In the coming week, continue to pray for all of the leaders mentioned in question #2 during our Caring Time. Next week we will look at the power of love to motivate Christians to live as Christ did on this earth, develop meaningful relationships with nonbelievers and lead them to prepare for Christ's return.*

Summary: Paul's concern here is how Christians relate to those outside the church. The general principles in 12:17–21 (e.g., don't resort to violence to "get even") are now given specific focus in this discussion of the relationship of Christians to civil authorities. Historical conditions that the original readers of this letter faced must be remembered. If we do not take their situation into consideration, then it is possible to teach more than Paul intended. In Paul's day, Rome was clearly a restraining force against chaos. Without some kind of control the Christians would surely have been eliminated by one of the many factions. Furthermore, it was crucial that Christians be seen as good citizens and not be expelled from Rome, as had the Jews because of a riot some years earlier (probably occasioned by Christ being preached in the synagogue).

Note, too, that Paul does not deal with the question of how Christians relate to a government gone sour, just as in Romans he doesn't tell Christians how to relate to an apostate church. Nor does he give any guidance as to how Christians should involve themselves in a participatory democracy. This was a specific word to particular Christians in a given era. Care must be taken in making modern applications, especially since in the book of Revelation Rome clearly appears to be pictured as having fallen under the control of evil, and Christians must then relate to it quite differently.

13:1 *Everyone.* That is, every Christian in Rome; no one is exempt. *submit.* This word is sometimes mistranslated "obey" (there are three Greek words for obedience). Submission must be understood in light of Romans 12:10 (honoring others above oneself) and Philippians 2:3–4 (counting others as better); Christians must recognize the claim that the authorities have upon them. However, there are times when God must be obeyed rather than men (Mark 12:13–17; Acts 5:29). *governing authorities.* Those authorities are established by God (Dan. 4:17, 25, 34–35).

13:2 *resists.* Literally, "has taken a stand against" what God has instituted. Such persons are actually rebelling against God, and will bring civil judgment or God's judgment on themselves.

13:3–4 Paul is not discussing governments that are unjust and which punish good works and praise evil.

13:4 *the sword.* Governmental force, properly used, helps prevent tyranny and executes justice; it brings punishment on the wrongdoer.

13:5 *conscience.* Since the Christian knows that God has appointed the ruler, to disobey would create a guilty conscience.

13:7 *taxes.* Local taxes such as duty, import/export taxes, taxes for the use of roads or for the right to drive a cart, etc. *tolls.* Any tribute, paid by members of a subject nation to Rome, consisting usually of three types: a general tax on agricultural produce, a 1% income tax and a poll tax paid by everyone between the ages of 14 and 65.

The Power of Love

Scripture Romans 13:8–14

LAST WEEK *The Christian's role in submitting to government authorities was our topic in last week's session. We were reminded that we should pray for and respect our leaders. Today we will look at the power of love. It is the motivation for Christians to live as Christ did on this earth, develop meaningful relationships with nonbelievers and lead them to prepare for Christ's return.*

 Ice-Breaker Connect With Your Group (15 minutes)

A common bumper sticker today says, "I owe, I owe, so off to work I go!" Paul tells us today that the only thing we should owe anyone is a debt of love. Take turns sharing your thoughts and experiences with owing something to others and paying your debt of love.

Leader
Welcome and introduce new group members. Choose one, two or all three Ice-Breaker questions, depending on your group's needs.

1. If you could have one of your debts paid in full right now, what would it be?

   ○ Mortgage.
   ○ Automobile loan.
   ○ School loan.
   ○ Credit card.
   ○ Personal loan.
   ○ Other _____.

2. If you could live anywhere you wanted and money was no object, where would you live?

3. In order to love your neighbors you have to get to know them. What are your neighbors like?

   ○ I never see them.
   ○ We share lawn equipment.
   ○ They're always inviting us over.
   ○ They're really good friends.
   ○ I have to watch out for them because they look suspicious.
   ○ Other _____..

Bible Study Read Scripture and Discuss (30 minutes)

God has us all here for a reason. He redeemed us to make our lives better, give us an eternal home and to take as many people with us as we can. Love that comes from God is the power source for us to be able to live as we should, and share Jesus with those who do not yet believe. Read Romans 13:8–14 and note how Paul describes the love we should have for others.

Leader
Select two members of the group ahead of time to read aloud the Scripture passage. Then discuss the Questions for Interaction, dividing into subgroups of three to six.

The Power of Love

Reader One: [8]Do not owe anyone anything,

Reader Two: except to love one another,

Reader One: for the one who loves another has fulfilled the law. [9]The commandments:

You shall not commit adultery,
you shall not murder,
you shall not steal,
you shall not covet,
and if there is any other commandment—all are summed up by this:

Reader Two: You shall love your neighbor as yourself. [10]Love does no wrong to a neighbor. Love, therefore, is the fulfillment of the law.

Reader One: [11]Besides this, knowing the time, it is already the hour for you to wake up from sleep, for now our salvation is nearer than when we first believed. [12]The night is nearly over, and the daylight is near, so let us discard the deeds of darkness and put on the armor of light. [13]Let us walk with decency, as in the daylight: not in carousing and drunkenness; not in sexual impurity and promiscuity; not in quarreling and jealousy.

Reader Two: [14]But put on the Lord Jesus Christ, and make no plans to satisfy the fleshly desires.

Romans 13:8–14

Questions for Interaction

Leader
Refer to the Summary and Study Notes at the end of this session as needed. If 30 minutes is not enough time to answer all of the questions in this section, conclude the Bible Study by answering question 7.

1. What was the occasion of your first debt or loan?

   ○ Money from a friend to buy candy.
   ○ Money for a date.
   ○ Automobile.
   ○ Engagement ring.
   ○ College.
   ○ Dream vacation.
   ○ Home.
   ○ Other _____.

2. What is one of the greatest examples of love you have ever witnessed?

3. How does "loving one another" fulfill the law (v. 8)? Who is our neighbor? How do we show "love" to our neighbors?

4. How does Christ's impending return affect the way you live your life? In what areas of your life should you make some adjustments to better prepare for his return?

5. Paul lists three major areas of sin in verse 13. In what other ways do we sometimes fall into the trap of trying to satisfy our "fleshly desires" (v. 14)?

6. How does one "put on the Lord Jesus Christ" (v. 14)? What are some practical ways that we can "walk with decency" (v. 13)?

   ○ Be courteous to others while driving and not give in to "road rage."
   ○ Avoid movies and materials that promote sexual impurity.
   ○ Talk problems out rather than quarreling.
   ○ Other _____.

7. What is one thing you could do this week to "put on Christ" in your life?

Going Deeper

If your group has time and/or wants a challenge, go on to this question.

8. How do we develop meaningful relationships with our lost neighbors while maintaining our personal convictions about lifestyle issues?

Caring Time Apply the Lesson and Pray for One Another (15 minutes)

For us to be able to "put on Christ," we need more than study—we need support and encouragement. This is your time to give that to each other. Share your responses to the following questions before closing in prayer.

1. What do you look forward to most about these meetings?

2. Who are the neighbors you would like for us to pray for?

3. In what real and practical way can you show love to a neighbor this week? (Refer to discussion from question 3 under the ions for Interaction.)

Leader
Have you identified someone in the group who could be a leader for a new small group when your group divides? How could you encourage and mentor that person?

NEXT WEEK *Today we looked at the power of love, and how it is the motivation for Christians to live as Christ did on this earth, develop meaningful relationships with nonbelievers and lead them to prepare for Christ's return. In the coming week, follow through on praying for and showing kindness in some way to a neighbor, family member or friend. Next week we will study how we are to relate to one another when we disagree over matters of personal conviction.*

Summary: Beginning in 12:1, Paul shifted his emphasis from theology to lifestyle. He first outlined how believers are to live as members of a Christian community (12:1–13). Then he looked at the question of how Christians are to relate to nonbelievers, ending that section with a very practical discussion of how Christians are to relate to the governing authorities (12:14–13:7). Here Paul moves from specific instructions on relationships to the general principle that guides all relationships: the law of love (vv. 8–10). He ends by pointing out what motivates Christians to follow this law of love—the imminent return of Christ. Paul's summary of the Christian life here in verses 8–14 is therefore: "Love others because the new age is dawning."

13:8 *owe.* A repetition in negative form of the positive statement in verse 7 ("Pay your obligations to everyone"). In verse 7, Paul has in mind public taxes, while here he turns to private debts.

13:9 Paul points to the second half of the Ten Commandments and indicates that each law would be automatically fulfilled if people kept the more basic principle that underlies them— loving others in the same fashion in which they love themselves. If a person really loved his neighbor, he wouldn't steal from him, etc. *neighbor.* In Leviticus 19:18, the neighbor is a fellow Jew; but the Parable of the Good Samaritan (Luke 10:25–37) expands "neighbor" to include all people. One's neighbor is the person in need, regardless of race or nationality.

13:10 Augustine once said, "Love God—and do what you like." If one truly loves, that person's life will automatically fall into those patterns established by the written Law. Still, since all people are sinful and imperfect, the admonitions of the Ten Commandments as well as those of Paul will be of great value in helping to clarify the path of love.

13:11–14 The idea of the Second Coming motivating believers to live morally can also be found in Matthew 25:31–46; Mark 13:33–37; Philippians 4: 4–7; 1 Thessalonians 5:1–11,23; Hebrews 10: 24–25; James 5:4–11; and 1 Peter 4:7–11.

13:11 *knowing the time.* This present age within which believers now live is not the ultimate reality. It is merely the prelude to a greater reality that will burst forth when Christ returns. Therefore Christians are not to live as if the here-and-now is all there is. Rather, remembering what Christ did in the past, they are to set their eyes on the future and live a life consistent with the coming new age. Thus, the Second Coming motivates one to moral living. The idea of the present age occurred previously in 3:26; 8:18; and 11:5. *sleep.* Sleep is inappropriate for those who must prepare for the imminent coming of Christ. *salvation.* Here understood as a divine event that will take place at a particular time in the future; i.e., though one enters into salvation upon conversion, this is a state to be realized fully only at the Second Coming.

13:12 *night.* The present age. *daylight.* The coming age inaugurated by Christ's second coming, in which God's new order will appear. *is near.* The early church understood that the life, death and resurrection of Jesus had ushered in the last days—the end time. God, however, because of his patience, had provided an interval before the culmination of the "night," the purpose of which is to allow other men and women to come to faith. During this interval the call to the Christian is to remain alert and expectant, knowing that the Second Coming may occur at any time. *armor of light.* That which one obtains from God and which is appropriate to wear when the new age dawns (Eph. 6:11–12).

13:13–14 In the summer of A.D. 386, Aurelius Augustine, Professor of Rhetoric at Milan University, sat weeping in a friend's garden, wanting to begin a new life but not knowing how, when he heard a child chanting, "Take Up and Read! Take Up and Read!" He picked up his friend's copy of Romans and read these two verses. "No further could I read," he later wrote, "nor had I any need; instantly, at the end of the sentence, a clear light flooded my heart and all the darkness of doubt vanished away" (Confessions). Thus is the conversion story of one of the early church's most influential theologians.

13:13 *carousing.* Originally referred to a group of supporters who accompanied home a victor at the games, singing his praises. It later came to have a negative sense, describing revelry or orgies. *drunkenness.* While all Greeks (including children) drank wine even at breakfast (when they dipped their bread into wine), drunkenness was considered a shameful thing. *sexual impurity.* Literally, "a bed." In the first century, prior to Christianity, chastity was almost unknown and was not considered a virtue by most people. *promiscuity.* The public display, without shame, of immoral acts. *quarreling.* The desire for power and prestige manifested by a willingness to stir up trouble if one is not in charge. *jealousy.* Envy that begrudges another's place or gifts.

13:14 *put on the Lord Jesus Christ.* To put on the armor of light (v. 12) is, in fact, to put on Christ. It is not merely a matter of cultivating Christian virtues independently on one's own merit.

Relating to One Another Over Personal Convictions

Scripture Romans 14:1–23

LAST WEEK *Last week we looked at the summary of all the commandments: "You shall love your neighbor as yourself" (13:9). We were reminded that our number one priority as Christians is to love. It is the motivation for us to live as Christ did on this earth, develop meaningful relationships with nonbelievers and lead them to prepare for Christ's return. Today we will study how we relate to one another over personal convictions. We will identify some governing principles we are to live by regardless of our personal convictions about certain "gray areas."*

 Ice-Breaker Connect With Your Group (15 minutes)

Leader
Choose one or two of the Ice-Breaker questions. If you have a new group member you may want to do all three. Remember to stick closely to the three-part agenda and the time allowed for each segment.

To eat or not to eat, that is the question! Many people have strong convictions about the food they eat, whether it be for health reasons, religious reasons or just personal likes and dislikes. Take turns sharing some of your convictions about food.

1. What is the toughest food or drink you have given up for a period of time? Why did you give it up?

   ○ Red meat.
   ○ All meat.
   ○ Solid food (fasting).
   ○ Sugar.
   ○ Certain beverages.
   ○ Other _____.

2. What was your favorite meal when you were growing up?

3. What is your favorite place to eat out?

Bible Study Read Scripture and Discuss (30 minutes)

Leader

Ask two members of the group, selected ahead of time, to read aloud the Scripture passage. Have one person read verses 1–11; and the other read verses 12–23. Then discuss the Questions for Interaction, dividing into subgroups of three to six.

Disagreement over personal convictions is a common thing in Christianity. Paul knew that he must address this issue right away, before it caused a lack of unity in the church. Our tendency is to stay away from people who do not believe just exactly like we do. As we are about to read in Romans 14:1–23, sometimes we have to agree to disagree but it should not change how we relate to each other as fellow Christians.

Relating to One Another Over Personal Convictions

Reader 1:

14 Accept anyone who is weak in faith, but don't argue about doubtful issues. [2]One person believes he may eat anything, but one who is weak eats only vegetables. [3]One who eats must not look down on one who does not eat; and one who does not eat must not criticize one who does, because God has accepted him. [4]Who are you to criticize another's servant? Before his own Lord he stands or falls. And stand he will! For the Lord is able to make him stand.[5]One person considers one day to be above another day. Someone else considers every day to be the same. Each one must be fully convinced in his own mind. [6]Whoever observes the day, observes it to the Lord. Whoever eats, eats to the Lord, since he gives thanks to God; and whoever does not eat, it is to the Lord that he does not eat, yet he thanks God. [7]For none of us lives to himself, and no one dies to himself. [8]If we live, we live to the Lord; and if we die, we die to the Lord. Therefore, whether we live or die, we belong to the Lord. [9]Christ died and came to life for this: that He might rule over both the dead and the living. [10]But you, why do you criticize your brother? Or you, why do you look down on your brother? For we will all stand before the judgment seat of God. [11]For it is written:

> As I live, says the Lord,
> every knee will bow to Me,
> and every tongue will give praise to God.

Reader 2: [12]So then, each of us will give an account of himself to God.[13]Therefore, let us no longer criticize one another, but instead decide not to put a stumbling block or pitfall in your brother's way. [14](I know and am persuaded by the Lord Jesus that nothing is unclean in itself. Still, to someone who considers a thing to be unclean, to that one it is unclean.) [15]For if your brother is hurt by what you eat, you are no longer walking according to love. By what you eat, do not destroy that one for whom Christ died. [16]Therefore, do not let your good be slandered, [17]for the kingdom of God is not eating and drinking, but righteousness, peace, and joy in the Holy Spirit. [18]Whoever serves the Messiah in this way is acceptable to God and approved by men. [19]So then, we must pursue what promotes peace and what builds up one another. [20]Do not tear down God's work because of food. Everything is clean, but it is wrong for a man to cause stumbling by what he eats. [21]It is a noble thing not to eat meat, or drink wine, or do anything that makes your brother stumble. [22]Do you have faith? Keep it to yourself before God. Blessed is the man who does not condemn himself by what he approves. [23]But whoever doubts stands condemned if he eats, because his eating is not from faith, and everything that is not from faith is sin.

Romans 14:1–23

Questions for Interaction

1. What "doubtful issues" do Christians argue about at times?

   ○ Drinking alcohol.
   ○ Dancing.
   ○ Entertainment preferences.
   ○ Day of worship.
   ○ Style of worship.
   ○ Clothing.
   ○ Other _____.

Leader
Refer to the Summary and Study Notes at the end of this session as needed. If 30 minutes is not enough time to answer all of the questions in this section, conclude the Bible Study by answering questions 6 and 7.

2. What does Paul mean by describing some believers as "weak in the faith" (v. 1)? When it comes to gray areas, how do you react to those who have strict convictions? Those with more lenient convictions?

3. According to Paul's teaching, how should we treat one another regardless of our convictions?

4. For those who are "strong" and can eat anything, what is the caution (v. 13)?

5. What is a "stumbling block"? Where does cultural influence come into play?

6. How do we find out if something we are doing is a "stumbling block" for another Christian? What should we do if another Christian's choices are causing us to stumble?

7. What sacrifices would you be willing to make so you don't cause a person weak in the faith to stumble?

Going Deeper   If your group has time and/or wants a challenge, go on to this question.

8. How can our personal convictions affect our relationships with nonbelievers? Should we compromise our beliefs so as not to offend someone?

Caring Time
Apply the Lesson and Pray for One Another (15 minutes)

Help each other in this Caring Time to be sensitive to each other's needs, regardless of personal convictions. Begin by sharing your responses to the following questions. Then take some time to share prayer requests and pray for one another.

Leader
Conclude the prayer time today by reading Isaiah 45:22–25, which includes the Scripture Paul quoted in today's reading.

1. On a scale of 1 (very weak) to 10 (very strong), how would you describe your faith this past week?

2. What have other Christians done in the past that has caused you to stumble? How do you need to forgive the people involved?

3. How can the group pray for you regarding the sacrifice you mentioned in answer to question 7?

NEXT WEEK *Today we looked at the dangers of criticism among those who are Christians. We identified some governing principles we are to live by regardless of our personal convictions about "gray areas." We were reminded to pursue righteousness, peace, joy and all that helps to build up one another. In the coming week, seek forgiveness from any fellow Christians you may have been a "stumbling block" to. Next week we will focus on the importance of unity and accepting one another in the Christian faith. We will see that Christ has given us mercy, love, peace, joy and the Holy Spirit to help us live in harmony with one another.*

Summary: While it is difficult to pin down the identity of the groups Paul addresses here, the general issue is quite clear. There were two perspectives at work in the church at Rome, and they threatened to split it apart. There were those who felt that in Christ all the old taboos, restrictions and ceremonial laws were done away with. These were the "strong," and to them all food and drink were alike and no day was sacred. On the other hand, the "weak" could not bring themselves to violate the regulations they had lived by for so long. Paul's sympathies are with the broad perspective (the strong), though he addresses most of his comments to "the strong," calling for sensitivity to the scruples of "the weak."

14:1 *Accept anyone.* This is the basic imperative addressed to the "strong" majority in the church: receive the "weak" into fellowship. *who is weak in faith.* Those who are not sure that their faith allows them to do certain things. The issue is not a lack of faith in Christ. Both the "weak" and the "strong" are authentically Christian. *don't argue.* Do not judge negatively the scruples of another.

14:2 *eat.* The Jews could not eat certain foods (Lev. 11), nor could members of certain Greek sects (e.g., the Pythagoreans abstained from meat).

14:3 *look down/criticize.* Two forms of judgment: the tendency of the "strong" not to take seriously the scruples of the weak (i.e., to laugh at them or even despise them); and the tendency of the "weak" to act superior and become censorious (because they felt that not doing certain things made them better Christians). Both attitudes are wrong. *God has accepted him.* The abstainer cannot condemn those who indulge, since no one can presume to judge a person God has accepted.

14:4 It is Christ himself who is concerned whether the "strong" Christian continues in faith or falls away.

14:5 *day.* The Jews observed various festivals and fasted on certain days each week. *con-*

vinced. Another principle guiding action: let action or abstinence result from conviction.

14:6-9 Both conclusions are arrived at out of a desire to serve God—for whom all Christians live.

14:10 *brother.* Paul reminds them of their true relationship with one another. This is a family issue—not a contention between strangers. Besides, God alone has the right to judge others. *judgment seat.* A Roman judge sat on a special seat dispensing justice.

14:13 This verse summarizes verses 9–12. *stumbling block.* A new theme is introduced into the discussion: the liberty of the strong can, in fact, be detrimental to others. What appears to them as an innocent pleasure or action may cause the more scrupulous pain, shock, outrage or even hurt.

14:14 *I know and am persuaded.* Paul comes down clearly on the side of the strong (Mark 7:15). *unclean.* That is, in the ritual sense: there is no food that has power to harm one's relationship with God. *considers a thing to be unclean.* For those believers who have not been convinced that Christ abolished the ceremonial law of the Old Testament (even though the food is not objectively unclean), it is subjectively so for that person.

14:15 If the "strong" exercise their liberty even when they know such actions are seen as sinful by the "weak," they are failing to act lovingly toward them. To do so is to jeopardize the faith of the weak and to disturb the harmony of the body. To act lovingly is more vital than to exercise one's freedom.

14:17–18 Such matters as eating or drinking are trivial in kingdom terms; to cause spiritual ruin over them is scandalous.

14:17 *righteousness, peace, and joy.* The kingdom of God does not consist of selfish actions, without regard for the scruples of one's brothers and sisters. Instead, the kingdom of God consists of "righteousness"—giving God and others their due (especially in this case, understanding and consideration), "peace"—that which makes for the highest good for another (especially here, right relationships), and "joy"—that which comes by seeking the good of others. Paul urges outward actions motivated by the needs of others, rather than a self-oriented insistence on personal "rights."

14:19 *builds up one another.* This includes helping either an individual Christian or the church grow in faith and practice.

14:21 The strong are called upon to use their strength not to eat or drink when doing so would cause harm. *drink wine.* The Old Testament does not forbid the drinking of wine except for priests on duty (Lev. 10:9) or Nazirites (Num. 6:2–3). Certain wine, however, may have been considered unclean, because its firstfruits had been offered as a libation to a pagan god.

14:23 *faith.* Here faith signifies a sort of inner freedom or liberty that comes from knowing that what one is doing is in accord with Christian faith in general. *sin.* When a Christian acts without that sense of inner liberty, such an act, even though in itself is neutral (neither inherently bad or good), is sin to that Christian. Strong Christians need to know this when they urge the weak to partake against their conscience.

Accepting One Another

Scripture Romans 15:1–13

> **LAST WEEK** *How should we relate to fellow Christians when we differ on personal convictions? That was our topic in last week's session, and we identified some governing principles we are to live by regardless of our personal convictions about "gray areas." Today we will study principles of accepting one another in the Christian faith and being in unity. As we will see, Christ is our example, and he has given us several things to help us live in harmony with one another.*

 Ice-Breaker Connect With Your Group (15 minutes)

God wants us to be filled with joy and peace as we go about our life trusting in him. Take turns sharing some things that bring joy into your life.

1. What do you like to do for fun?

- ○ Read.
- ○ Play video games.
- ○ Watch TV.
- ○ Listen to music.
- ○ Party.
- ○ Do nothing.
- ○ Camp.
- ○ Hike.
- ○ Sports.
- ○ Hang out with friends.
- ○ Be alone.
- ○ Go on a trip.
- ○ Walk in the woods.
- ○ Extreme sports.
- ○ Shop.
- ○ Other _____.

Leader
Choose one, two or all three Ice-Breaker questions, depending on your group's needs.

2. Who do you like to share your fun times with?

- ○ Spouse.
- ○ Children.
- ○ Parents.
- ○ Close friends.
- ○ Anybody.
- ○ Nobody.
- ○ A date.
- ○ A group.
- ○ This group.
- ○ Other _____.

3. What is your favorite season of the year?

- ○ Fall.
- ○ Winter.
- ○ Spring.
- ○ Summer.

 # Bible Study Read Scripture and Discuss (30 minutes)

Leader
Select two members of the group ahead of time to read aloud the Scripture passage. Then discuss the Questions for Interaction, dividing into subgroups of three to six.

Paul continues to stress the need for accepting and building up our fellow Christians. We don't always feel like accepting some people, but acceptance of others is a characteristic that should define those who follow Christ. We can't let disagreements get in the way of unity within the body of Christ. Read Romans 15:1–13 and note that the way we accept others is through the power of the Holy Spirit.

Accepting One Another

Reader One: **15** Now we who are strong have an obligation to bear the weaknesses of those without strength, and not to please ourselves. ²Each one of us must please his neighbor for his good, in order to build him up. ³For even the Messiah did not please Himself. On the contrary, as it is written,

Reader Two: The insults of those who insult You have fallen on Me.

Reader One: ⁴For whatever was written before was written for our instruction, so that through our endurance and through the encouragement of the Scriptures we may have hope. ⁵Now may the God of endurance and encouragement grant you agreement with one another, according to Christ Jesus, ⁶so that you may glorify the God and Father of our Lord Jesus Christ with a united mind and voice.

⁷Therefore accept one another, just as the Messiah also accepted you, to the glory of God. ⁸Now I say that Christ has become a servant of the circumcised on behalf of

the truth of God, to confirm the promises to the fathers, [9]and so that Gentiles may glorify God for His mercy. As it is written:

Reader Two: Therefore I will praise You among the Gentiles,
and I will sing psalms to Your name.

Reader One: [10]Again it says:

Reader Two: Rejoice, you Gentiles, with His people!

Reader One: [11]And again:

Reader Two: Praise the Lord, all you Gentiles;
all the peoples should praise Him!

Reader One: [12]And again, Isaiah says:

Reader Two: The root of Jesse will appear,
the One who rises to rule the Gentiles;
in Him the Gentiles will hope.

Reader One: [13]Now may the God of hope fill you with all joy and peace in believing, so that you may overflow with hope by the power of the Holy Spirit.

Romans 15:1–13

Questions for Interaction

Leader
Refer to the Summary and Study Notes at the end of this session as needed. If 30 minutes is not enough time to answer all of the questions in this section, conclude the Bible Study by answering questions 6 and 7.

1. In what ways has someone made sacrifices for you? How have you made sacrifices for others?

2. What does Paul mean by "bear the weaknesses of those without strength" (v. 1)? In what ways are we to accept one another? Is there anyone we should not show acceptance to?

3. Paul prays that believers would have a united mind and voice (vv. 5–6). What does he mean in light of the last passage where he talked about agreeing to disagree?

4. Paul quotes several beautiful passages in this reading. How do the Scriptures encourage and give us hope? What passage of Scripture have you found to encourage you?

5. What do these phrases from verse 13 mean to Christians? to nonbelievers?

   ○ "God of hope."
   ○ "Joy and peace."
   ○ "Overflow with hope."
   ○ "The power of the Holy Spirit."

6. What was your life like before you realized Christ's acceptance of you?

7. Where do you need acceptance or hope in your life right now?

Going Deeper | If your group has time and/or wants a challenge, go on to this question.

8. Who is the "root of Jesse" (v. 12)? What is the new position of the Jews in light of this revelation of the Gentiles acceptance by God?

Caring Time Apply the Lesson and Pray for One Another (15 minutes)

Rejoice in your salvation together and join in a time of sharing and prayer "with a united mind and voice" (v. 6). After responding to the following questions, share prayer requests and close with a group prayer.

1. How have you seen the Holy Spirit at work in your life this past week?

2. What principle or truth did you hear in this lesson that you really needed today?

3. How can the group pray for you regarding what you shared from question 7?

Leader
Conclude the prayer time today by asking God for guidance in determining the future mission and outreach of this group.

NEXT WEEK *Today we looked at the principles of accepting one another in the Christian faith and being in unity. Christ is our example to follow, and he has given us mercy, love, peace, joy and the Holy Spirit to help us live in harmony with one another. In the coming week, ask the Holy Spirit to help you bring unity to your church. Next week we will learn the heart of Paul as he concludes this letter to the Romans.*

Summary: This is the concluding paragraph of Paul's argument in the book of Romans. For one last time before he draws his book to a close, Paul asserts the amazing fact (to a first-century Jew) that the Gentiles are part of God's plan. He cites four Old Testament passages from the Septuagint (the Greek Old Testament) to demonstrate that Jesus came for the sake of both Jew and Gentile. Each shows the Gentiles coming to faith. From the previous study, we know that the Jews struggled with this truth. We also know that division existed in the Christian faith over minor issues. Paul writes to both of these issues by emphasizing the principles of unity.

15:1 *not to please ourselves.* This is not a general admonition to avoid all that personally pleases us (as it has been misinterpreted), but rather a call to the strong not to please themselves by exercising their rights to indulge when it might hurt others.

15:3 Paul quotes Psalm 69:9, in which Christ is understood to be saying to God that those insults directed to God have fallen on him. This is an example of how far Christ went in not pleasing himself.

15:4 This explains and justifies Paul's use of an Old Testament reference by way of application to Christ. One of the values of the Old Testament to Christians is that it promotes hope. When Christians hold fast to their hope for the future, it is a stimulus to appropriate action in the present.

15:5–6 Paul's wish for the Christians at Rome is put into the form of a prayer.

15:6 *united mind and voice.* Literally, "to think the same." This is a unity of inward feeling and outward expression.

15:7 *accept one another.* Paul's basic command addressed to the church as a whole, by which he sums up 14:1–15:13. It is broader than the exhortation in 14:1, which is directed to the strong.

15:9–12 *As it is written.* These quotations are taken from all three divisions of the Old Testament—"the Law of Moses, the Prophets and the Psalms" (Luke 24:44)—and from three great Jewish heroes: Moses, David and Isaiah. The first quotation (v. 9) is from David's song of deliverance (2 Sam. 22:50; Ps. 18:49); the second (v. 10), from Moses' song to the people of Israel (Deut. 32:43); the third (v. 11), from both the shortest and the middle chapter of the Bible (Ps. 117:1); and the fourth (v. 12), from Isaiah's messianic prophecy (Isa. 11:10).

15:12 *root of Jesse.* The Messiah would be descended from David, whose father was Jesse.

15:13 Paul ends with a prayer that Christians will experience the triple gift of joy, peace and hope. The source of these gifts is the Holy Spirit. Division in particular destroys joy and peace. In this closing benediction Paul uses all the key words from chapters 1–8: hope, joy, peace, trust (faith) and power (of the Holy Spirit). Thus he concludes his argument.

Paul's Heart for Souls

Scripture Romans 15:14–33

LAST WEEK *"Now may the God of endurance and encouragement grant you agreement with one another" (15:5). This was the prayer Paul had for the Romans as he emphasized the importance of Christian unity in last week's Scripture passage. We also looked at how Christ has given us mercy, love, peace, joy and the Holy Spirit to help us live in harmony with one another. Today we will learn that the heart of Paul is for nonbelievers everywhere to hear and believe in Jesus.*

 Ice-Breaker Connect With Your Group (15 minutes)

Paul traveled many places during his missionary journeys. As he finished this letter, he wrote of his plans to visit Rome. Take turns sharing what travels you have been on along your life journey.

Leader
Choose one, two or all three of the Ice-Breaker questions, depending on your group's needs.

1. Where is the last place you went on vacation? Share the best and worst part of that trip.

2. What country would you like to visit? What countries have you already visited?

3. How many times have you moved in your life? What is the hardest thing about moving?

 Bible Study Read Scripture and Discuss (30 minutes)

Paul had a purpose for his life and he knew what it was. He was an incredible pioneer of our faith and didn't let anything distract him from his missionary zeal. Today we want to remind ourselves of our ultimate purpose as followers of Christ, no matter what our vocation in life is. Read Romans 15:14–33 and note how Paul desires to be with his brothers and sisters in Christ.

Leader
Select a member of the group ahead of time to read aloud the Scripture passage. Then discuss the Questions for Interaction, dividing into subgroups of three to six.

Paul's Heart for Souls

[14]Now, my brothers, I myself am convinced about you that you also are full of goodness, filled with all knowledge, and able to instruct one another. [15]Nevertheless, to remind you, I have written to you more boldly on some points because of the grace given me by God [16]to be a minister of Christ Jesus to the Gentiles, serving as a priest of God's good news. My purpose is that the offering of the Gentiles may be acceptable, sanctified by the Holy Spirit. [17]Therefore I have reason to boast in Christ Jesus regarding what pertains to God. [18]For I would not dare say anything except what Christ has accomplished through me to make the Gentiles obedient by word and deed, [19]by the power of miraculous signs and wonders, and by the power of God's Spirit. As a result, I have fully proclaimed the good news about the Messiah from Jerusalem all the way around to Illyricum. [20]So my aim is to evangelize where Christ has not been named, in order that I will not be building on someone else's foundation, [21]but, as it is written:

> Those who had no report of Him will see,
> and those who have not heard will understand.

[22]That is why I have been prevented many times from coming to you. [23]But now I no longer have any work to do in these provinces, and I have strongly desired for many years to come to you [24]whenever I travel to Spain. For I do hope to see you when I pass through, and to be sent on my way there by you, once I have first enjoyed your company for a while. [25]Now, however, I am traveling to Jerusalem to serve the saints; [26]for Macedonia and Achaia were pleased to make a contribution to the poor among the saints in Jerusalem. [27]Yes, they were pleased, and they are indebted to them. For if the Gentiles have shared in their spiritual benefits, then they are obligated to minister to Jews in material needs. [28]So when I have finished this and safely delivered the funds to them, I will go by way of you to Spain. [29]But I know that when I come to you, I will come in the fullness of the blessing of Christ.

[30]Now I implore you, brothers, through the Lord Jesus Christ and through the love of the Spirit, to agonize together with me in your prayers to God on my behalf: [31]that I may be rescued from the unbelievers in Judea, that my service for Jerusalem may be acceptable to the saints, [32]and that, by God's will, I may come to you with joy and be refreshed together with you.

[33]The God of peace be with all of you. Amen.

Romans 15:14–33

Questions for Interaction

1. In this study of Romans, what "bold point" has God made with you that you want to share with this group?

2. What did God accomplish through the ministry of Paul? How has God accomplished his work through your life?

3. Paul's aim was to "evangelize where Christ has not been named" (v. 20). What have you learned from Paul on how to spread the Gospel in your city and around the world?

Leader

Refer to the Summary and Study Notes at the end of this session as needed. If 30 minutes is not enough time to answer all of the questions in this section, conclude the Bible Study by answering questions 6 and 7.

4. What is the church's obligation to the "poor among the saints" (v. 26)? How do we facilitate that in the life of a growing church?

5. Who agonizes in prayer for you? Who do you agonize in prayer for?

6. How do your ambitions compare with Paul's?

   ○ I have the same clarity and sense of purpose.
   ○ My main concern is to see people come to a saving faith in Jesus.
   ○ I have a heart for souls and the poor.
   ○ My ambitions don't begin to compare with Paul's.
   ○ Other _____.

7. Where do you sense God calling you in furthering his kingdom?

   ○ Praying for the world.
   ○ Helping the poor.
   ○ Sharing my faith story with my neighbors and professional associates.
   ○ Assisting in ministries at my church.
   ○ Other _____.

| **Going Deeper** | If your group has time and/or wants a challenge, go on to this question. |

8. Who were the "unbelievers in Judea" that Paul wanted to be rescued from and why did he need to be rescued? Who do you need to be rescued from and why?

Caring Time Apply the Lesson and Pray for One Another (15 minutes)

Following Paul's example, let us help each other in this time of prayer. Begin by sharing your responses to the following questions. Then share prayer requests and concerns and close in a group prayer.

1. How do you feel about this small group? How has it "refreshed" (v. 32) you on your journey of faith?

2. What can you do in the coming week to encourage your pastor?

3. What would you like to see God accomplish in your life?

Leader
Following the Caring Time, discuss with your group how they would like to celebrate the last session next week. Also, discuss the possibility of splitting into two groups and continuing with another study.

NEXT WEEK *Today we were inspired as we considered the heart that Paul had for souls, both those he had already reached with the Gospel and those he had yet to evangelize. God accomplished a great deal through Paul, and he wants to do the same through us. Our job may be as an accountant, teacher, nurse, etc., but we all have a role in sharing the Good News. In the coming week, take a bold step and talk about Jesus to that person God has laid on your heart. In our final session next week, we will focus on Paul's final remarks to the church in Rome.*

Notes on Romans 15:14–33

Summary: Paul brings his letter to a close (prior to his postscript in chapter 16 in which he greets various friends) by discussing: (1) his apostleship and his authority to write as he does (vv. 14–22), and (2) his travel plans—to go first to Jerusalem (to deliver a collection for the poor) and then to Spain, stopping en route in Rome (vv. 23–33). Paul has been made a minister to the Gentiles. He has faithfully fulfilled this calling and has seen fruit from his ministry. But all he will talk about is what Christ did through him. This is why he refers to "the power of miraculous signs and wonders, and by the power of God's Spirit," which brought about belief in Christ on the part of the Gentiles. The collection for the poor in Jerusalem is on the order of a debt for Paul. When he was commissioned by the church to be the apostle to the Gentiles, the only request they had was that he remember the poor (Gal. 2:10). This was no new concern. Once before, he and Barnabas had brought a gift to Jerusalem from the Christians in Syrian Antioch (Acts 11:29–30; 12:25). Such a gift could aid the unity between Jewish and Gentile Christians, as well as model the appropriate response to human need.

15:14 These are not words of flattery designed to win over a hostile audience. One sentence would hardly suffice in light of the preceding chapters. Rather, he seems to feel that to write such specific instructions for behavior (as he has done in 12:1–15:13) to a church he has never visited might seem overly bold (v. 15), even presumptuous. So he hastens to assure them that indeed he does consider them to be mature Christians. **full of goodness.** They love one another, frankly and sincerely. **filled with all knowledge.** They understand God's truth— what the Gospel is and what it requires. **able to instruct.** Of sound moral and intellectual character, they can work out their own problems; i.e., correcting the wrong in one another and encouraging each other to righteous living.

15:15 boldly. Paul's words might appear bold, in that he had neither founded nor visited the church in Rome. He may fear, especially, offending either of the two groups (the weak and the strong) referred to in 14:1–15:13. **on some points.** Probably 12:1–15:13, in which he addresses specific issues of Christian behavior.

15:16 a minister. In Greek, the word is *leitourgos*, the word from which "liturgy" is derived. In its original use, it designated patriotic tasks voluntarily undertaken on behalf of Greece, such as financing a choir, training an athletic team, or paying the expenses of a naval warship; i.e., "generous service." By God's grace (v. 15), Paul is such a minister, and his responsibilities include writing as he has done to the Romans.

serving as a priest. Paul speaks of his role as a minister in priestly terms: The Gentiles are the offering he presents to God. The Holy Spirit has made them pure and sanctified them. His is a holy service, similar to that of the Jewish priests.

15:19 *signs and wonders.* See Acts 2:22,43; 4:30; 5:12; 2 Corinthians 12:12 and Hebrews 2:4. *Illyricum.* A Roman province on the eastern coast of the Adriatic Sea. Paul has preached throughout the northeastern Mediterranean, establishing churches in the major cities. Although no specific mention is made elsewhere of ministry here, it could well have come in A.D. 55 or 56 (2 Cor. 2:12–13), when Paul was in Macedonia (which shared a border with Illyricum).

15:20 Paul's call is to be a pioneer missionary.

15:22 The demands of such pioneer missionary activity have thus far prevented a visit to Rome.

15:23 Paul is not saying that there is no further work to be done there, but simply that his presence is no longer required, since the pioneer work has been completed.

15:24 *Spain.* The Roman colony of Spain was situated at the edge of the civilized world—no doubt the reason that Paul's pioneering spirit was drawn there. Still, it was no cultural backwater. The poet Lucian came from there, as did Seneca, the Stoic philosopher, and the emperors Trajan, Hadrian, and Theodosius I. Although Paul was arrested and imprisoned prior to realizing the plans he outlines here and there is no New Testament record that he ever went to Spain, he just might have achieved his goal. An ancient document written in Rome (c. A.D. 95) states that, prior to his martyrdom, Paul "came to the extreme limit of the West," which is almost surely Spain. *hope to see you.* Among other reasons, Paul has written this letter as a means of introduction to the church in Rome, which he hopes will support his missionary activity in Spain. Though he does not specify what assistance he hopes for, it probably included material aid as well as prayer and fellowship, and perhaps even a companion from the church who was knowledgeable about Spain.

15:26 *Macedonia and Achaia.* Two Roman provinces located south of Illyricum, on a peninsula bordering the Adriatic and Aegean Seas (in the region of modern Greece). These were not the only territories that contributed (Acts 20:4; 1 Cor. 16:1). They are probably mentioned because at the time that Paul wrote Romans he was living in this region. *to the poor ... in Jerusalem.* Whether it was because of prejudice or because of generally hard economic times in Judea that the Christians there were especially in need is unknown.

15:27 *pleased.* Their gift was voluntary; the obligation was a moral debt, not a legal levy by the mother church. The fact that Gentiles have been grafted into the blessings which originally belonged to Israel was Paul's point in 11:11–14.

15:31 Paul has experienced hostility from unbelieving Jews as well as suspicion from converted Jews, the latter over his ministry to the Gentiles.

Paul's Final Words

Scripture Romans 16:1–27

LAST WEEK *In last week's session, we were inspired by Paul's heart for souls. His main goal in life was to spread the Gospel to anyone who would listen. We are also to be open to God's plan for us and to have the same heart for souls that Paul had, regardless of our vocation. Today we will conclude this study of Romans with a look at Paul's final remarks to the church in Rome.*

Ice-Breaker Connect With Your Group (15 minutes)

Paul ends his letter to the Romans with many personal greetings. Take turns sharing your own experiences with keeping in touch with family and friends.

1. Is it harder for you to "say hello" (make new friends) or to "say good-bye" (release old friends)?

2. When was the last high school reunion you went to? How did you feel? If you didn't go, explain why.

3. What family member or friend would you like to see that you haven't seen in a long time?

Leader
Begin this final session with a word of prayer and thanksgiving for this time together. Choose one or two Ice-Breaker questions to discuss.

Bible Study Read Scripture and Discuss (30 minutes)

Paul shows us his emotions here in this final chapter as he writes his personal greetings to his friends in Rome. This gives us a rare glimpse into his driven and caring personality. Read Romans 16:1–27 and note what a beautiful community these Christians had.

Leader
Select a member of the group ahead of time to read aloud the Scripture passage. Then discuss the Questions for Interaction, dividing into subgroups of three to six.

Paul's Final Words

16 I commend to you our sister Phoebe, who is a servant of the church in Cenchreae. ²So you should welcome her in the Lord in a manner worthy of the saints, and assist her in whatever matter she may require your help. For indeed she has been a benefactor of many—and of me also.

³Give my greetings to Prisca and Aquila, my co-workers in Christ Jesus, ⁴who risked their own necks for my life. Not only do I thank them, but so do all the Gentile churches.

⁵Greet also the church that meets in their home.

Greet my dear friend Epaenetus, who is the first convert to Christ from Asia.

⁶Greet Mary, who has worked very hard for you.

⁷Greet Andronicus and Junia, my fellow countrymen and fellow prisoners. They are outstanding among the apostles, and they were also in Christ before me.

⁸Greet Ampliatus, my dear friend in the Lord.

⁹Greet Urbanus, our co-worker in Christ, and my dear friend Stachys.

¹⁰Greet Apelles, who is approved in Christ.

Greet those who belong to the household of Aristobulus.

¹¹Greet Herodion, my fellow countryman.

Greet those who belong to the household of Narcissus who are in the Lord.

¹²Greet Tryphaena and Tryphosa, who have worked hard in the Lord.

Greet my dear friend Persis, who has worked very hard in the Lord.

¹³Greet Rufus, chosen in the Lord; also his mother—and mine.

¹⁴Greet Asyncritus, Phlegon, Hermes, Patrobas, Hermas, and the brothers who are with them.

¹⁵Greet Philologus and Julia, Nereus and his sister, and Olympas, and all the saints who are with them.

¹⁶Greet one another with a holy kiss.

All the churches of Christ send you greetings.

¹⁷Now I implore you, brothers, watch out for those who cause dissensions and pitfalls contrary to the doctrine you have learned. Avoid them; ¹⁸for such people do not serve our Lord Christ but their own appetites, and by smooth talk and flattering words they deceive the hearts of the unsuspecting.

¹⁹The report of your obedience has reached everyone. Therefore I rejoice over you. But I want you to be wise about what is good, yet innocent about what is evil. ²⁰The God of peace will soon crush Satan under your feet. The grace of our Lord Jesus be with you.

²¹Timothy, my co-worker, and Lucius, Jason, and Sosipater, my fellow countrymen, greet you.

²²I Tertius, who penned this epistle in the Lord, greet you.

²³Gaius, who is host to me and to the whole church, greets you. Erastus, the city treasurer, and our brother Quartus greet you.

[²⁴The grace of our Lord Jesus Christ be with you all.]

²⁵Now to Him who has power to strengthen you according to my gospel and the proclamation of Jesus Christ, according to the revelation of the sacred secret kept silent for long ages, ²⁶but now revealed and made known through the prophetic Scriptures, according to the command of the eternal God, to advance the obedience of faith among all nations— ²⁷to the only wise God, through Jesus Christ—to Him be the glory forever! Amen.

Romans 16:1–27

Questions for Interaction

Leader
Refer to the Summary and Study Notes at the end of this session as needed. If 30 minutes is not enough time to answer all of the questions in this section, conclude the Bible Study by answering question 7.

1. Who in the group would you like to thank for encouraging you, as Paul encouraged his brothers and sisters in Christ? In what ways did this person help you?

2. What kind of things does Paul commend in the persons mentioned in verses 1–16? What does this say about what really matters in life?

3. Apparently Paul had several great friendships. What does it take to make those kinds of friends?

   ○ A lot of time and effort to keep in touch.
   ○ A committed and loving heart.
   ○ Putting my friend's needs above my own.
   ○ Other _____.

4. What does Paul warn the believers about in verses 17–18? What could this mean for us today?

5. What is meant by "be wise about what is good, yet innocent about what is evil" (v. 19)? How does that apply to us today?

6. How can God exercise his power "to strengthen you" (v. 25)?

7. What will you do to continue to grow in Christ in the coming weeks?

Going Deeper   If your group has time and/or wants a challenge, go on to this question.

8. Paul seems to give great value to women in the church. What do you think is the role of women in the church?

Caring Time   Apply the Lesson and Pray for One Another (15 minutes)

Gather around each other now in this final time of sharing and prayer and encourage one another to have faith and hope as you go back out into the world.

Leader
Conclude this final Caring Time by praying for each group member and asking for God's blessing in any plans to start a new group and/or continue to study together.

1. What was your serendipity (unexpected blessing) during this course?

2. What was the high point for you in this study of Romans? What will you take with you?

3. How would you like the group to continue to pray for you?

Notes on Romans 16:1-27

Summary: Paul ends his letter with a list of greetings, giving a fascinating glimpse into the first-century church.

16:1 *I commend ... Phoebe.* It is likely that Phoebe carried Paul's letter from Corinth to the church at Rome. (The government postal service was used only for official purposes.) Typical in letters of his day, Paul includes a note of commendation in which he makes two requests: that they receive Phoebe as a sister in the Lord, and that they assist her because she has helped many others. Phoebe was probably a woman of wealth and influence. She is a Gentile Christian, since no Jewess would have been named, as she was, after a pagan deity. *servant.* Literally, "deaconess." From the way Paul speaks of her in verse 2 and from the gift mentioned in Romans 12:7 (the word "service" is derived from the same root as "deacon"), her ministry was probably that of helping others, especially the poor and needy. *church.* Surprisingly, the first occurrence of this word in Romans. *Cenchreae.* One of the two seaports that served the city of Corinth, located seven miles east on the Saronic Gulf.

16:3–5a *Prisca and Aquila.* Aquila, a Jew born in Pontus in Asia Minor, and his wife Prisca (or Priscilla) appear regularly in the New Testament. They are first mentioned when they are living in Corinth (Acts 18:1–3) as a result of having been banished from Rome along with other Jews in A.D. 52 (because of an edict by the emperor Claudius). Paul lived with them there for 18 months. Both Paul and Aquila were tentmakers by trade. When Paul left Corinth for Ephesus, Prisca and Aquila went with him (Acts 18:18). At Ephesus, Prisca and Aquila were responsible for instructing the brilliant Apollos in the Christian faith (Acts 18:24–26). From Ephesus they sent greetings from the church in their house back to Corinth (1 Cor. 16:19). Now they are in Rome once again, Claudius' edict having elapsed. When this couple is mentioned in the New Testament, generally Prisca's name is noted first, contrary to the custom of the day. It has been speculated that she might have been by birth an aristocratic Roman woman (due to evidence related to her name), in which case her marriage to a humble Jewish tentmaker would be living proof of how Christ destroyed barriers of race, rank and class.

16:5 *the church ... in their home.* During the first two centuries, there were no special church buildings, so Christians met in the homes of their members (1 Cor. 16:19; Col. 4:15; Philem. 2).

16:6 *Mary.* Probably a Jewish woman.

16:7 *Andronicus and Junia.* Probably husband and wife. It is significant that one of the early apostles was a woman. The feminine form of the word is quite common, while the masculine form of the word is nonexistent. *apostles.* In the general sense, these were people commissioned by Christ (either in person or through the church) to establish new churches.

16:8 *Ampliatus.* A common slave name. In a Roman cemetery belonging to Damatilla, niece of the emperor Domitian, there is an elaborate tombstone with this name on it—an indication that perhaps a noble household had been influenced by the Gospel and that a slave had become a person of significance in the church.

16:10 *Apelles.* A common Greek name, often used by Jews. *household of Aristobulus.* This might be the Aristobulus who was a grandson of Herod the Great. Upon his death, his servants and slaves became the property of the emperor, known by their former master's name—among whom were a number of Jews.

16:11 *Herodion.* A common name in Herod's household, perhaps a member of the Aristobulus group, known personally by Paul. *household of Narcissus.* Since Narcissus is not greeted, he is either a deceased Christian or a pagan. The name may refer to a notorious secretary to the emperor Claudius, who amassed a huge fortune as a result of bribes paid him to ensure that petitions reached the emperor. He was forced to commit suicide when Nero came to the throne, and his household became a part of the imperial household.

16:12 *Tryphaena and Tryphosa.* Probably twin sisters. *worked hard.* This phrase means "to labor to the point of exhaustion," in contrast to the names of these women, which mean respectively "dainty" and "delicate"—perhaps an intentional pun by Paul. Each time he uses the phrase "work hard" in this chapter, it is in connection with women: Mary in verse 6, Tryphaena and Tryphosa here, and Persis in verse 12b. In most other cases when Paul uses this word (*kopiac*), it refers to his labor as a minister of the Gospel, and so it may well have that meaning here too. *Persis.* Literally, "Persian woman."

16:13 Rufus. Quite possibly the son of Simon of Cyrene, who carried Jesus' cross. Simon is identified (in Mark 15:21) as the father of Alexander and Rufus, an unusual description unless the sons were known in the place where the letter was directed. Mark's Gospel was written for the Roman Christians.

16:14 The five men here are probably either slaves or freed men.

16:16 *a holy kiss.* The kiss was a common greeting used by Christians as part of their worship service. It may have been the custom to exchange kisses in preparation for communion. Years later, Origen wrote about this verse: "From this injunction and several similar ones the custom has been handed down to the churches, that after the prayers, the brethren shall greet one another in turn."

16:18 *smooth talk.* A word used to describe a person who speaks well but acts badly.

16:19 *wise about what is good, yet innocent about what is evil.* Untainted by evil. The word is used to describe pure metal (or milk) containing no hint of a foreign substance (*kakon*). The word for "innocent" is *akeraios*, "unmixed, simple, pure." In Greek it was used of wine that was not diluted and of metal that was not weakened in any way.

16:20b *The grace of our Lord Jesus be with you.* Typically the sender of the letter wrote out this subscription in his or her own hand.

16:22 *Tertius.* The only time the name of one of Paul's secretaries is revealed.

16:23 *Gaius.* This name is mentioned several times in the New Testament. It probably refers to the Gaius mentioned in 1 Corinthians 1:14, with whom Paul was staying in Corinth while he wrote Romans.

16:25–27 This closing doxology is a single complex sentence in which God is praised for the salvation he offers in Christ Jesus.

16:25 *sacred secret.* In the New Testament, this refers to truths about God's plan that were unknown until God disclosed them. They are insights about God that could not be achieved through reasoning or deduction (1 Cor. 1:18–20), but are known solely because God has revealed them.

16:26 As Paul has shown throughout the letter, the Gospel was foretold in the ancient writings (Rom. 1:2; 15:4) although it could not be comprehended until the advent of Christ. *to advance the obedience of faith among all nations.* This is the goal of the Gospel, it is for all nations, not just for the Jews. All are invited to become the people of God.

Personal Notes

_____

_____

_____

_____

_____

_____

_____

_____

_____

_____

_____

Personal Notes

Personal Notes

_____

_____

_____

_____

_____

_____

_____

_____

_____

_____

_____

Personal Notes

Personal Notes

Personal Notes

Personal Notes

_____

_____

_____

_____

_____

_____

_____

_____

_____

_____

Personal Notes